GW01465810

HOW TO ENJOY YOUR WORK

HOW TO ENJOY YOUR WORK

...and have fun doing it!

DICK LEATHERMAN

First published in the United States of America in 1990 entitled *Is Coffee Break the Best Part of Your Day?* by HRD Press Inc, 22 Amherst Road, Amherst, Massachusetts 01002, USA.

This edition first published in Great Britain in 1991 by Kogan Page Ltd, 120 Pentonville Road, London N1 9JN

British Library Cataloguing in Publication Data
A CIP record for this book is available from the British Library.

ISBN 0-7494-0461-2

Typeset by AsTec, Newport, Saffron Walden, Essex
Printed in Great Britain by Clays Limited, St Ives plc

Contents

Acknowledgements 6

Introduction 7

1. **The Attitude Opportunity** 9
2. **How to Benefit from Criticism** 17
3. **Communication – Are You Listening?** 24
4. **Working Effectively with Others** 46
5. **How to Receive Work Assignments** 55
6. **How to Solve Problems** 59
7. **Making Good Decisions** 78
8. **The Importance of Planning** 89
9. **Managing Your Time** 103
10. **Managing Your Performance Appraisal** 114
11. **It's *Your* Career** 130
12. **Meeting Change Creatively** 149
13. **Being Managed** 160
14. **Conclusion** 165

Further Reading From Kogan Page 167

Acknowledgements

Grateful acknowledgement is made to the following individuals who read the rough draft of this book and then offered valuable ideas to make the final version even better: Del Boerner, Joanne DeMark, Ken Grieve, Leonard Hill, Linda Herrig, Jim Houlditch, Dennis and Dianne LaMountain, Denise Leblond, Robert Newman, Roger Pelkey, Mohan Rao, Steve Rouch, Carol L Smith, Charlie Sweet, Arlan Tietal, Deirdre Weisbach, Craig Woodacre.

And special thanks to: David McKnight for his herculean efforts in proofing my grammar, syntax, and punctuation; Bill Griffin, Professor of English, Virginia Commonwealth University, for the final editing of this manuscript; Shirley Foutz, Literacy Specialist, Richmond Newspapers, and Betsy Weaver, Chesterfield County Schools, for their work in making this book more readable.

My thanks also to Nancy Leatherman, MD, wife and friend. From her I have learned much about life – which is what this book is all about.

Introduction

If you're tired of feeling that work is drudgery, then this book is for you. It's a distilled, boiled-down explanation of how you can become the best you can be – and have fun doing it! But there is a catch. You'll no longer be able to blame your feelings about your job or your performance on your organisation, boss, or colleagues. Why not? Because *you* are responsible for the joy you find in your work! Not your boss, colleague, or spouse. You!

Something interesting begins to happen when you really take responsibility for yourself. You work better. You become more effective. And when you become as productive as you can be, you will find that work becomes a pleasure. It's a wonderful cycle. The better you perform, the more you will enjoy what you do. And the more you enjoy your work, the better you become at it. And what's more – society rewards people who become more effective at what they do.

Sure, life could always be easier. Bosses could be better bosses. The organisation probably could make some changes that would make your job less difficult. But as long as you expect others to change, you won't do much about yourself. And there *are* things you can do almost immediately to become an outstanding employee – no matter what kind of crazy organisation you work for. And when you become an outstanding employee, you don't have to work for crazy organisations. You can work anywhere you want to – and enjoy it!

There are two things that will make your job more fun. One is to know as much as you can about the job. The second is to be effective. By 'effective' I mean an employee who uses his or her head, has good work habits, and gets along with others. Job knowledge and effectiveness – its takes both to be successful. And successful people are the ones who make their jobs fun.

There are exceptions, of course. If you are the only person in your organisation who can operate the old computer that was installed 20 years ago, then you don't have to be particularly effective in dealing with others – until the day that they replace that old computer. But *outstanding* employees need not only to learn their job, they also need to learn how to be effective.

Sometimes we're fortunate in being able to learn how to be effective by having a competent boss or effective parents. But many of us aren't so lucky. We may even have had incompetent bosses or less than effective parents. So we have never had the opportunity to learn what it means to take responsibility for ourselves, to become the best that we can be. That's what this book is all about.

I remember my first job – as a plumber's mate. How I hated that job! But I became pretty good at unclogging stopped-up loos, digging ditches and threading pipe. In other words, I learnt to do the job. But I was still a lousy employee! I sloped off, took long tea breaks (tea breaks were definitely the best part of my job), even longer lunch breaks, and always looked for ways of getting out of doing work. The only reason I kept the job that summer was because the owner was my uncle.

The following summer, my mother persuaded him to take me back. This time, I was assigned to work with Jack. Jack was the hardest-working person I'd ever seen – and one of the happiest. Forced by necessity to keep up with him, I became more productive. And as I became more productive, I began to feel great satisfaction in being competent. And the more competent I became, the more I enjoyed my job. So from Jack, I learned what it really meant to work. Not in terms of job knowledge; I already knew how to do the job. Jack taught me work habits. He became my model of what it meant to work. And what I learned that summer many years ago has become a deep part of me ever since.

So this book is for those of you who never had a chance to work for a 'Jack'.

Chapter 1
The Attitude Opportunity

You can't smell or taste an attitude. Attitudes are intangible. But most people know instinctively what good – and bad – attitudes 'look' like. You recognise attitudes by what people say or do. In general, if they speak well about their organisation and their jobs, they are showing a good attitude. If their work shows little effort because they don't care about their job, they probably have a bad attitude.

What you see in others are symptoms. Often, it is difficult really to know what is going on inside them. You see their behaviour, draw conclusions about their attitudes, and even guess how they are feeling. But all too often you don't know *why* they feel the way they do.

However, you can look inside yourself. It isn't always easy; but you can frequently work out why you feel the way you do. If you think you might have an 'attitude opportunity' – if you feel there's room for improvement in your attitude to work – here is a six-step method you can use to understand what is going on – and remedy it. And at the end of this chapter, there are work sheets you can use to help you improve your attitude.

First, here is an overview of the six steps. Ask yourself the questions:

1. What am I doing?
2. How did I feel?
3. Why did I feel like that?
4. What am I going to do?
5. How do I monitor my progress?
6. How do I reward myself for changing?

Now, let's look at each of these steps in more detail.

1. What am I doing?

What are you doing that might make someone say, 'You really do have an attitude problem'? Write down your answer. Be as specific as possible. It might help to ask yourself: 'What are the things I do or say that show my attitude needs improving?' You may need to list several things to describe your attitude problem.

If you are not sure what to write, ask some of your colleagues how they see your attitude towards your job. This can be both easy and difficult. It's easy because all you have to do is ask the right person – your boss, or a trusted friend who knows you and your job performance. But it can also be hard to ask another person for constructive criticism. It's hard because it may force you to face something you might not want to face. And it's hard because most people simply don't like getting negative feedback.

Part of the answer lies in how you ask for feedback. If you ask, 'Do I seem to have a bad attitude to my job?' the focus is on the negative side of your behaviour. A better question is, 'Can you think of any ways I could improve my attitude at work?' This is a positive way of asking the same question – and it will produce positive suggestions rather than a review of your negative behaviour.

When you get an answer to your question, do your best not be become defensive. You simply want the truth – not a chance to explain yourself to others. Listen. Avoid interrupting. And ask for examples to help the person giving the feedback to be more specific. Then, if possible, ask a second key person the same question to see if he or she has similar suggestions.

2. How did I feel?

When you did – or said – the things described in Step 1 above, how did you really feel? Angry? Hurt? Depressed? Write these feelings down. Sometimes Step 2 is harder than you might think. Things happen, and if your feelings about them are not expressed or get buried, it may be hard to work out later exactly what you are feeling. Sometimes you will need help with this – try speaking to a friend or relative who's a good listener.

3. Why did I feel like that?

Now write your answer to this question. You may feel as you do for a number of reasons.

1. You may feel strongly about something because of something similar that has happened in the past.
2. You may feel a certain way because of certain events happening outside your work.
3. Or your attitude may in fact be a reaction to the way your organisation is operating. Let's look at each of these in turn.

Past experience. Your past experiences in life affect the way you see things today. In fact, such experiences can have a great impact on your present feelings. But the past may not be in your conscious thoughts, even though you are affected by it. So when you first attempt, to answer the question, 'Why do I feel the way I do?' you will most often think of recent events. And these events are usually what somebody or something did to you.

But if you give yourself time to think more deeply, you may be able to remember a similar situation that occurred in your past – even in your childhood. This is not to say that a recent event isn't an important cause of your feelings. But the *intensity* of your reactions can sometimes only be fully explained by a similar negative experience – or experiences – at a previous time in your life.

Here is a personal example:

> Many years ago, I took a field sales job at a company. After several years went by, I had developed what anybody would have said was a 'bad attitude'. I was late turning in my monthly expense forms. And there were days when I didn't even make my sales calls. I didn't stay at home, because I would have been embarrassed to admit to anyone that I had a problem with my job. So I'd either force myself to make sales calls on old accounts where I felt accepted, or just go somewhere and get a cup of coffee.
>
> When I ask the 'Why?' question – Step 3 above – it is obvious why I didn't like the work I was doing. I didn't enjoy making sales calls because:
>
> 1. I felt as if I was 'imposing' on my clients; and
> 2. I couldn't stand the frequent rejection – which I took personally.
>
> I was sensitive to feelings of rejection because, as a chubby teenager, my secondary school years were miserable. I was late in developing physically and I walked the corridors in

fear of being bullied by the bigger boys. Later, I began to see that there were other boys who didn't get harassed even though they weren't muscle men. They were the nice ones – the popular boys. So I made a career out of being nice. And it worked. I no longer got bullied in the corridors.

As a young salesperson, I still felt a little like the fat schoolboy. I wanted to be liked, and the way to be liked was to be nice to people. But sometimes my customers weren't very nice. They didn't buy my products, for whatever reason – and I took it personally!

Why didn't I give up? There were two reasons, one obvious and one hidden. First, there was a small part of my job that I really enjoyed – training new sales people. And because I enjoyed that part of my job, I spent quality time in preparing and conducting on-the-job training with them. But the real reason I didn't give up my job concerned my father, who was a salesman.

A sales career was something I admired about my father – and later thought he admired in me. That made it hard for me to accept the fact that I really wasn't cut out for it.

So past experience had led to a career choice that had placed me in a job I didn't like – and at that time I didn't understand the real cause of my attitude problem.

Fortunately, the story had a happy ending. I wasn't sacked. I was promoted – to a full-time training job that I really enjoyed, and performed well!

Outside causes. Many things that cause an 'attitude problem' have nothing to do with the job itself. For example, if you are experiencing a marital separation or divorce, or even if you've just has a bad fight with your spouse, it's hard to be excited about your job. If your on-the-job attitude is a result of a serious problem off the job, it is best to get help. Talk to someone you trust and who will listen to you. Or check to see if your organisation has an employee assistance scheme. There is nothing shameful about seeking help when you are faced with what seems to be an overwhelming problem.

Organisational causes. In some cases, your organisation can cause problems. For example, I once worked for an individual who encouraged cheating on company expense vouchers. I was told to 'hide' a legitimate business expense by claiming that it was something other than what it really was. Even though the company was not actually being cheated, I didn't feel good about it. But my boss insisted I do it anyway. As a result, even though he was in many ways a competent manager, my negative attitude towards him made it difficult for me to accept his advice and counsel in other areas.

In another case, I know an employee whose work values are different from those of his organisation. He feels that working 45 hours a week is more than enough. But his organisation has no qualms about asking him to work 50, 60 or even 70 hours a week. This individual is *not* going to change his organisation's values. And he cannot accept working 60 or more hours per week. As long as he continues to stay with this organisation, he will have difficulty with his attitude.

After considering why you feel the way you do, the next step is to take action to resolve the situation by turning it into an opportunity.

4. What am I going to do?

In some cases, taking action will simply mean deciding to change your external behaviour – and you may have to make an effort. If you seldom get to work on time in the morning, then start coming to work on time! If you are a constant moaner, then stop complaining. This may sound too simple. But for the most part, you *do* have control over what you do or say. And you *can* take responsibility for your outward symptoms – and create an opportunity for positive change!

Sometimes, simply changing your outward behaviour can produce such good results that you may not need to dig deeper to find other causes for an attitude problem. But more often, if you are looking for a permanent solution to a problem, you will need to understand better what you are feeling, why you are feeling it, and then take action to remedy the underlying causes of the problem. In my case, the trouble was solved when I was promoted to a job I immediately liked. But suppose I hadn't been promoted? Knowing what I know now, the best way for me to have handled my situation would have been to consider more deeply the 'What?' and 'Why?' of my negative feelings – and then to share with my father what I had discovered about myself. I know now that he would have been flattered by my reason for choosing a sales career. He would have advised me to look for a job I enjoyed doing. And he would have felt pleased that I chose to confide in him.

5. How do I monitor my progress?

Your goal here will be to build habits that will help you to maintain constant improvement. Since by now you have a good understanding of the behaviour that needs improvement, it will be easy to measure your progress towards correcting it. For example, if you are consistently late for work, and decide to be on time in the future, keep an attendance log in your desk diary for several months, noting the time when you arrive at work each day. You may even want to strengthen your commitment by sharing your plans with your boss or colleague.

6. How do I reward myself for changing?

Reward yourself when you change your behaviour for the better. If you tell your supervisor you plan to make a change, and do so – then tell him or her when you have successfully reached your goal. Or pick a trusted friend, tell him or her about your plans, and ask for positive feedback when you show a changed attitude.

A good attitude towards your job is essential for success and satisfaction – and for happiness at home! If you suspect that you have an opportunity to improve your attitude, do something about it. If you don't the person who is hurt the most is you. The simple steps above will literally work miracles in changing bad attitudes to good ones, and frustration to job happiness.

The attitude opportunity check sheet

1. What am I doing?

A. What am I doing (or not doing), and saying (or not saying) that may be perceived as an 'attitude problem'? I'll need to be specific.

____

____

____

B. What have others said about my attitude?

____

____

C. Whom could I ask to give me honest feedback?

____

D. What question(s) could I ask this person? (For example, 'What specific things should I do or say that will demonstrate an improved attitude?' Remember to word the question so as to receive positive suggestions, not negative criticism. Ask for examples.)

____

____

____

E. Write a summary of what this individual says.

____

____

____

____

2. How did I feel?

When I originally did or said what I wrote in Step 1A above, how did I really feel?

____

____

3. Why did I feel like that?

____

____

____

What experience or experiences have I had in the past that may have influenced the way I felt?

____

____

____

4. What am I going to do?

What action(s) will I take to eliminate the symptoms (behaviour) of my past attitude?

____

____

____

If I have found an underlying cause of my attitude, was it an external cause or an organisational cause? __________

Given that I have identified the cause, what can I do to resolve the situation?

____

____

____

5. How do I monitor my progress?

How do I plan to monitor my progress as I change my attitude?

____

____

____

6. How do I reward myself for changing?

How do I plan to reward myself when I successfully change?

____

____

____

Chapter 2

How to Benefit from Criticism

> '**Ox · y · mo · ron:** a figure of speech in which opposite or contradictory ideas or terms are combined (eg, thunderous silence, sweet sorrow).'

Like the example above, 'constructive criticism' is a figure of speech that tends to appear contradictory. 'Criticism' often is, or appears to be, destructive – not constructive. You get 'destructive criticism' from family, friends, peers and bosses. It happens in meetings, in the corridor, over the phone and in your own home. There's no escaping it! Therefore, you need to cope with criticism in ways that will make it constructive.

In this chapter, the person who gives the criticism will be discussed, as well as your role as the receiver of the criticism. You will also see a step-by-step method for handling criticism. And finally, there is a work sheet at the end of the chapter that you can use to evaluate the times when you feel criticised.

The sender

Let's look first at the sender, or giver, of criticism. You know that it makes a great difference *who* is criticising you. But even more important than who is criticising you is their *motive* for doing so. If you sense that they are not motivated by a sincere desire to help, you probably won't listen to what they have to say. If they are angry, for instance, you may feel angry in response. Or if they normally criticise everything and everybody, you may question the validity of what they say. And if you sense that their motive is to prove you're 'wrong', you won't be very receptive.

When you are criticised can also make a difference. You have probably had days when you felt overloaded and stressed beyond your ability to cope. Criticism given at this time may seem almost more than you can bear.

Finally, *where* the criticism takes place can also have an impact on how you receive it. For example, criticism given in front of others is usually much harder to accept than if it is expressed in private.

The receiver

How well you handle criticism can depend on the perceived motive of the sender, when the criticism is given, and where it occurs. But come it will - and then what? How do you make the best of criticism?

First, remember that you do have the right to say 'No' to criticism. For example, if the time or place is truly inappropriate, then you can ask the sender to keep his or her comments for a more suitable time or place. You might say, 'Thank you for pointing that out. Since I feel uncomfortable with others present, would it be possible to finish this discussion later?' If it is your boss who is criticising you in front of others, it may sound a bit cheeky to ask your boss to continue his or her criticism at another time or place. But in most cases, this suggestion will be accepted.

Second, the problem of dealing with criticism is that there is usually a bit (or even more than a bit!) of truth in what the sender is saying. And if you care about what is being said, it is that bit of truth that hurts. For example, a friend of mine was raised at a time when the 'man' was the 'head of the household'. The man's responsibility was to provide for his family. So even though his wife earned a good living, he was sensitive to his 'traditional' role of supporting the family - through hard work. Therefore, if he spent a working day doing non-work-related activities, he felt a little uneasy. After all, by his values he should be working to support his family.

Recently, when his wife asked him to take a day off to do something with her, his reaction was, 'Oh no, that's a *working* day!' She felt rejected and a little angry and responded by saying, 'You took a day off last week to do what *you* wanted to do. So why can't you take a day off to do what *I* want to do?' Because what she said was partly true, he got upset. It took him a while to calm down and accept what she said, and agree to take the day off.

Now let's look at some ways you can manage criticism in the workplace.

First, accept that what you do in the face of criticism is up to you. You are seldom going to change the way others give you criticism. (Not that it can't be done; but it isn't likely.) Therefore, it's often easier to manage your own reactions to the criticism than it is to manage the way the sender is giving it.

Second, realise also that the criticism is true as perceived by the other person. It is rare for people to criticise without believing in the correctness of their criticism.

Third, it is also true that people will sometimes be irritated, or even angry, when giving criticism. A person may well be upset at being put in a position of having to criticise you. In addition, he or she may well have been criticised by his or her boss. 'After all,' the other person thinks, 'I don't need this hassle! I've got enough to do without having to put up with a problem that you have created.'

But to become angry because someone else is angry won't help. Instead, you need to handle the criticism in a way that will help you to understand what you have actually done, what you shouldn't have done (or didn't do that you should have), and what you need to do to correct the situation.

Finally, if you really want to take the responsibility for your own development, seek out criticism (or feedback) from others. In other words, act positively, be 'proactive', do not always be reactive. By appropriately asking others, you will be able to control who gives you feedback, where and when it occurs, and the subject of the feedback.

Handling criticism

Now let's look at some strategies for handling criticism constructively when emotions are strong.

1. *Listen! Listen intently.* And as you listen, look at the person who is criticising you. Don't think of what you are going to say in response to what you are hearing. Simply look, listen – and don't interrupt.

   Listening is the most powerful strategy you have for handling criticism. It's powerful for three reasons.

   - The more the other person talks, the more information you will have.
   - The more he or she talks, the lower his or her level of emotion will be. (Try this strategy the next time someone is irritated or angry with you. Notice how hard it is for that person to stay angry – if you simply listen without interrupting.)
   - If you realise that what you should do at this point is listen,

you won't waste energy getting angry or thinking about how you can best defend yourself.

2. *Paraphrase what you believe you heard.* If you can repeat, in your own words, what you think you heard, you will communicate clearly that you really did listen to what was said – and that you understood it. If you did *not* understand the criticism, the other person will let you know by giving you more information, or simply by repeating the original criticism. This will also give you time to mentally relax, listen carefully, and further reduce your level of emotion.

   For example, suppose my boss, Bill, walks into the office stops at my desk and says, 'Dick, you have the untidiest desk in the department. It always looks like a pig sty. Look at the appalling example you set for your subordinates! How can you expect people to keep their areas clean when your desk looks so disorganised?'

   Let's look at the facts. First, my desk *is* untidy. In fact, it's usually untidy (though not always – I remember clearing it up six months ago). None of my subordinates' desks are untidy. They are generally well-organised, and their desks are normally neat and clean. But I am also the best manager my boss has, and my untidy desk has not interferred with my production or leadership.

   So my instinctive response to my boss's criticism is to say, 'Now wait just a minute! My desk isn't *always* untidy. The last time I cleared it you didn't say a word. You didn't even notice. And not only that, all four of my people keep their desks cleaner than yours! So how can it be that my people are modelling their desk habits after me – or you?'

   The point here is that you can almost always find some element of untruth in the criticism, and attack that part of what was said. But don't do it! Arguing your case may work well in a courtroom, but it won't help in handling constructive criticism. It only makes the other person feel that you are not taking seriously what he or she has said – which will usually raise his or her emotional level.

   It would be far better for me to listen intently, without interrupting. Then I can paraphrase what I heard by saying, 'Bill, I can see you are very upset over the condition of my desk, because you feel that a good manager should be a good model for his subordinates. Is that correct?'

Notice that I acknowledged his feelings ('I can see you are very upset'), stated in my own words what he was upset about ('the condition of my desk'), rephrased why he felt upset ('a good manager should be a model for his subordinates'), and closed by asking if what I heard was correct ('Is that correct?'). My response had four components:

1. Acknowledgement of observed feelings
2. A restatement of the criticism
3. The reason(s) why he or she was upset
4. A question to confirm my understanding.

Notice also that I did not become defensive. I did not even attack that part of his statement that was incorrect (ie, I did not mention the fact that my subordinates' desks, all neat and clean, had not been affected by my 'appalling example').

3. *If necessary, ask questions to gain more information.* In the illustration above, for example, I could have asked for more specific information about the untidy desk, and then asked more questions about what he expected the desk to look like. Questions like, 'What in particular about my desk bothers you the most?' or, 'How, specifically, do you want my desk to look?' In the example above, of course, I knew what he meant by 'untidy desk'; and I also knew what he wanted it to look like! So I didn't need to ask information questions. Instead, I moved directly to Step 4.

4. *Ask 'action' questions.* Action questions probe for ideas about what should be done to correct the problem. In the example above, I might ask questions like, 'What ideas do you have about how I can keep my desk cleaner?' Or, 'What suggestions do you have about how I could organise my desk so that it doesn't get untidy?' Of course, I may already have seen how to correct the problem. But involving the other person in developing a solution communicates clearly my desire to change my behaviour.

5. *Commit yourself to doing something.* Make a decision to do at least one important thing to remedy the situation. In the above example, I could agree to begin by removing the stack of papers that always sits in the middle of my desk. There are

probably a number of things I can do to improve my desk. And whatever I do will take time. But if I commit myself to doing one key thing to improve the situation, there is a much better chance that I will be inspired to take the next step, and the next, and the next, until the goal is achieved.

6. *Devise ways to ensure that the change is permanent.* People are creatures of habit: they tend to revert to old ways of doing things unless there are built-in strategies to prevent this from happening. For example, there are a number of things I could do to ensure my success in my clean desk project. I could bet my subordinates £10 that I could keep my desk clean for a month (they would love to take my money). Or I could take a 'before and after' picture of my desk, and post it on the notice board. Do whatever works; and what works depends on you!

Receiving criticism is not easy. But if you remember that there is probably some truth in the criticism you receive, you can resolve to understand that truth and make the required changes.

How to benefit from criticism check sheet

Think of the last time someone criticised you. Analyse below how you handled the criticism.

1. How well did I listen without interrupting? ________________
____
____

2. Did I paraphrase what I thought I heard? ________________
If 'yes,' did I:
- Acknowledge the other person's feelings;
- Restate the criticism that I heard;
- Describe the reasons why he or she was upset;
- Ask a question to confirm the accuracy of my response? ____

Did I refrain from becoming defensive?________________
From attacking perceived weaknesses in the criticism?________

3. Did I ask questions to gain more information?________________
What questions did I ask?________________
____
____

4. Did I ask questions to involve the giver of the criticism to develop a solution that is suitable for both of us?____________
____
What questions did I ask?________________
____
____
If not, what questions could I have asked?________________
____
____

5. Did I commit myself to doing something?________________
Did I commit myself to doing too much?________________
What should I have committed myself to do?________________
____
____

6. If I committed myself to doing something, has the change become permanent?________________
If not, what can I do to ensure that the change is permanent?
____
____

Chapter 3

Communication – Are You Listening?

Speaking and listening: two major components of communication – and of life! And yet how few of us have had formal training in these two all-important areas. We've studied history, maths, English, physics, geography. But who ever had a 'speaking' book? And how many hours did we spend doing 'listening' homework? So how can we learn to communicate? Mostly from life's experiences. Good experiences. Bad experiences.

Experience has taught us what to do and what not to do. Unfortunately, not all the habits we acquire when learning to communicate are necessarily the most effective ways of doing it. Since this is such a critical skill, it is important that we look at how we communicate at the moment – and be willing to modify our behaviour if need be.

Although numerous books are available on the subject of communications in business, the majority were written for speakers, counsellors, supervisors and managers. And most of those few aimed at employees are very basic. The following helpful ideas are directed specifically to you, and they take a different approach!

You communicate with two main groups on the job – your bosses and your colleagues. Conversations with bosses are usually 'situational' – that is, they reflect the situation you are in. For example, you talk to your boss when being appraised, receiving assignments, being advised about a performance problem or reviewing career goals. These types of situation are covered in detail in other sections of this book. The purpose of this chapter is to examine how you communicate with your colleagues.

There are a number of ways to look at oral communication. But for our purpose, we will use a model to help explain what communication is. By using a model, we can establish a language to talk about – and understand – the way people communicate. A model can also help those of us who, like me, learn better graphically.

Let's first look at the three primary elements in the model, the 'Sender', 'Message', and 'Receiver'.

In its simplest form, the model shows that (1) someone (2) says something (3) to somebody. I wish it were that simple. But it isn't! People are infinitely complex and so are their communications. For example, last night I heard my wife say, 'Great!' I said, 'What's "great"?' She replied, 'I can't find my letter opener anywhere and I've just used it!' I thought 'great' meant something wonderful had happened. She said 'great' because she was irritated.

As you can see from the detailed model below, communication is a very complicated process. Not only is there a sender, message and receiver, there's also the situation or environment (when, where and how the communication occurs), and the feedback that one person received as he or she talks and then listens to another.

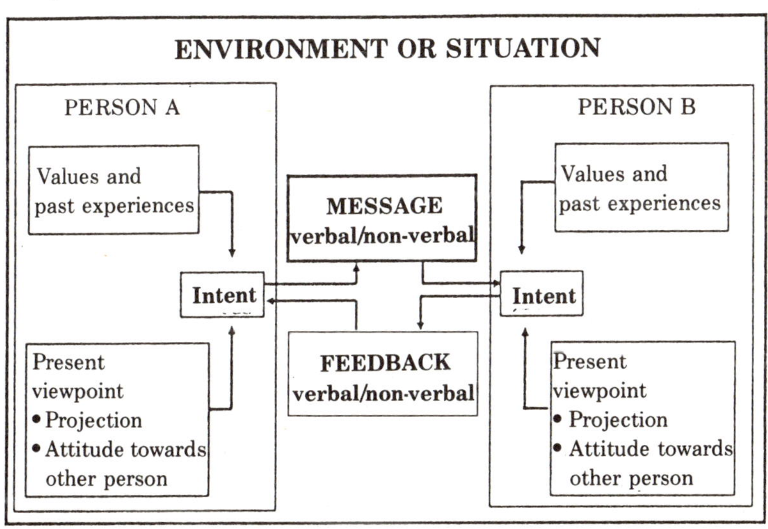

Using this model as a guide, we'll first look at the individuals involved in their communication with each other (values, past experiences, etc), then the 'message' itself, and last the way feedback affects communication.

So let's look at each of these three elements in more detail.

The sender and receiver

The message someone sends depends on his or her intent, which in turn depends on the individual's values, past experience, present perceptions, attitude towards the other person, and language skills. And all of this depends on the situation (the environment) that surrounds the sender. That's a lot of 'depends'!

Values and past experiences

To understand why some communication is not effective, you can look at your personal values. Values are those beliefs that are personally important to you in life. For example, I value my family over my work, but I value my work over other activities like watching TV or jogging. Values are strongly affected by the culture you grow up in – and by your age, sex, ethnic group or race. Differences in age can be an especially important factor. For example, a woman I know went back to further education after raising a family. She took some degree-level science courses (though she already had a master's degree in social work), then applied to do medicine and was accepted. She currently holds the unique honour of being the oldest woman ever to graduate from the medical faculty at her university.

But now, while doing her houseman's year at a local hospital, she finds it very difficult to maintain effective communication and working relationships with many of her fellow junior doctors. And her difficulty isn't due to her sex; many of the other residents are female. The problem lies mainly in the fact that she is in her late forties, while most of her colleagues are in their twenties.

This age difference affects her ability to communicate in two ways. First, she has had considerable experience in life that her colleagues have not had: she has married, had children, raised a family, worked in a variety of jobs, and experienced the death of a parent. For these reasons, she lacks common ground with most of her colleagues. If raising and establishing a relationship with your children is one of the most important areas in your life, how much of this can you really share with those who have not yet had children? In short, this woman is simply at a different stage in life from her professional peers – and she has greatly different interests.

But also, she grew up at a different time from that of her colleagues, and was taught a different set of work values. For example, she feels strongly that being a parent for her children was a higher priority than her career. Many of her colleagues feel just as strongly that becoming a doctor has the highest priority. The resulting conflicts with some of her colleagues are inevitable. And they sometimes obstruct effective communication between them.

The above example illustrates that the closer you are in age to your colleagues, the more likely it is that you will have effective communication with them. But age difference is not the only cause of communication difficulty. Because our society still rewards boys (and later, men) for their interest and participation in sports, you more often see groups of men, rather than women, sitting around talking about last night's big match. Conversely, women have had unique sets of experiences that men haven't had, and these sex-related differences and interests can inhibit good communication with men.

Other differences - such as further education versus non-further education experience, high versus low income, and minority versus non-minority status - can all interfere with effective communication. The fewer life experiences you have in common, the more different your values will be. And differing values tend to make communication more difficult.

When your values are not the same, it doesn't mean you can't communicate. But it does mean that communication requires special attention. When values are different, you have an even greater responsibility to follow good communication practices.

Having noted how important values and past experiences are in communicating, the next thing to examine is the sender's viewpoint as he or she communicates.

Present perceptions

The sender of a message will often communicate from his or her own viewpoint rather than from that of the person to whom the message is sent. This occurs because of two major reasons: the projection of one person's feelings on to another, and the attitude of one person towards another person.

Projection

If I see my world as me, then I will tend to see others as extensions of me. If, for example, there is something that I fear, then I am apt to think that others will also have the same fear. And if they don't fear what I fear, then I am likely to think there is something wrong with them.

Or, if there is a part of me that I don't like, then I am likely to expect to see that same thing in others. In other words, If I am secretly ashamed of a small part of me that is dishonest, I probably believe that others are also dishonest in the same way – even if they aren't.

Projections can create a lack of acceptance of one person by another, and thus cause communication problems. Let's look at an example. Bill, a new employee in the parts department of a large motor company, was assigned to work with Joe, a senior employee. Joe was asked by the supervisor to help Bill learn the ropes. Joe was a perfectionist. During the first day, Joe spent a significant amount of time telling Bill what he was doing wrong, and did not mention any of the things that Bill did right. It's likely that Joe had some feelings of dissatisfaction unrelated to Bill and thus focused on the negatives of Bill's work rather than the positives. By the end of the day, Bill was feeling bad about himself, Joe, and the job. As a result, Bill withdrew and did not communicate with Joe, and didn't learn the job as quickly as he should have done.

Attitude of one person towards another

My attitude towards you will definitely affect the way I relate to you. If you and I have had trouble dealing with each other in the past, I am likely to have difficulty not only in speaking to you, but also in listening to you.

Let me give you a personal example. I once had an unpleasant experience with an individual who is a senior human resource development specialist. But because of his expertise in proofing and editing, I put aside my negative feelings towards this person and asked him to be one of the reviewers of this book. Many of the comments that he wrote on the first draft of this book struck me as sarcastic and, even in some cases, cruel. But because his suggestions were excellent, I swallowed my pride (my initial reaction was to tell him where he could put his comments) and made the corrections that he offered. But I avoided any personal telephone calls with him even when, on occasions, I should have phoned him to clarify a comment that I didn't understand.

However, as time went by, my original negative feeling lessened and I began to see his comments in a different light. Instead of sarcasm, I saw remarkable humour. Instead of cruelty, I saw an individual who could bluntly say what needed to be said about a piece of poor writing. Today, I am thankful that I asked him to be a reviewer, I am pleased that he said yes, and I deeply appreciate his contributions. You see, he didn't change – I did. And my change in attitude had a strong and positive effect on our communication.

But I could have handled the situation better than I did. Rather than discovering that I felt better about him only as time went by, I could have taken the initiative and talked to him about my feelings. You see, the attitude we have towards another person is often a result of underlying feelings – feelings like anger, joy and sadness. Powerful words. Some people seem to be more inhibited about using such words at work than some four-letter words. And yet, simply talking to others about your feelings can often reduce the intensity of your emotion.

So rather than deal directly with feelings, some people find it easier to use a distant 'they' or 'them', and 'I'm very unhappy about what *they* did!' or 'I'm really angry with *them*!' What is much more difficult is, 'I'm really angry with you!', 'I am very unhappy about what you've done!' or 'I'm glad you are my friend.' One solution is to express your angry/glad/sad feelings without using the word 'you'. You might feel more comfortable saying, 'I am (state your feelings) because (state whatever happened or will happen).' For example, 'I'm happy because we've been assigned to work together'; or, 'I'm angry because I had to finish this job by myself even though we were both assigned to do it!'

We are not as direct as we should be for a number of reasons. Sometimes we are afraid. And when we are fearful, we may get angry. So we develop 'rituals' that protect us from others – or from ourselves. Here are some common types of ritual.

'Nothing'

Example: suppose that you and I are friends. A couple of days ago, I thought you were upset with me and I didn't know why. So I asked you what was wrong. You said 'Nothing'. But I could tell by your expression that you were really upset. At this point, we have a serious communication problem. By saying 'nothing', you have bottled up your anger and I don't have an opportunity to try to resolve the problem. And if you remain angry in order to punish me for whatever I (or somebody else) did or didn't do, then we will continue to have a communication problem. In fact, the problem gets worse, because now I become upset. I'm angry with you for not being honest with me, and for not giving me a chance to explain my point of view or to make amends – or simply to listen as your friend.

Kidding around

David and Peter are good friends who avoid confronting each other over problems because they are afraid. They're afraid of what *might* happen to their relationship if they are direct with each other. So they use humour and joke together, in the hope that the other one will 'get the message'. The end result, however, is that one never knows exactly how the other feels – and thus is never really able to resolve problems that arise between them. Or there may be times when the other person gets the message and is hurt by it. The hurt creates anger which is suppressed in order to protect the relationship. This suppressed anger adds another weight to their relationship and may put a wall between them. Communication and trust will be diminished.

The agreeables

Two colleagues are good friends. They work together and play together – but they don't fight together. So they often play a game called 'Agreeable', It works like this: if they both want something, but only one can have it, they each try to persuade the other to take it. It is almost comical to watch them as one says, 'Oh no, Bill, you take it' to which Bill responds, 'Oh, I wouldn't dream of taking it, because I know how much you really want it.' Then Steve says, 'What a wonderful friend you are! But there is no way that I could take it, since I know how important it is for *you* to have it!' To which Bill responds, 'Well, Steve, that is very nice of you, but . . .'

Each has good reasons to want what he wants. But neither can ask directly for it. So each one bends over backwards being 'kind' and 'considerate', depending on the other one to read his mind and satisfy his need. As a result they may spend days trying not to make mistakes that will hurt their relationship.

Dancing

Have you ever watched two people 'dance around' an issue because they are afraid to tackle it head on? Or maybe they're dancing because they don't know what really bothers them – so all they do is talk around the issue. The problem with dancing is that although it may be entertaining, it doesn't get anywhere.

Here is a real-life example of a married couple we will name 'Sue' and 'John', who finally stopped dancing around a serious issue.

John has a hard job which Sue hates - with a passion. Last week, she was again bitterly complaining about the job's long hours (50 to 60 per week), the long drive (two hours per day), the stress and pressure, and the fact that John gets called out at all hours of the night to handle emergencies (a couple of times a week). John responded by saying 'I know all these things bother you. But what's really troubling you?' Suddenly, Sue thought of her father, who had died from a heart attack, partially as the result of a stressful job. She said, 'I don't want you to die like my father did.'

The true cause is now clear. They could move towards a solution based on the real cause of the problem - a fear of death. If Sue sees John's job only as a problem of long hours spent commuting, then one solution is to move closer to the job. Or if she see that problem as the long working hours, then a solution is to find another job; or to cut down the hours by taking on an assistant. But if the real cause of Sue's distress is her fear of losing him, then they can look to solutions like, 'Select the best ways to keep John healthy.'

Rituals such as 'nothing', 'kidding around', the 'agreeables' and 'dancing' are poor - and finally destructive - substitutes for openly facing our problems with others. Direct communication of our feelings, done tactfully but without avoiding the issue, is almost always the best way to achieve good working relationships with others. Good communication results from honesty and believing in the ability of others to work constructively with us when they truly know how we feel.

At this point, the factors that affect the sender have been presented - factors like the person's values and past experience, and his or her present perceptions. Now we'll look at the message itself.

The message

What the other person hears you say (verbal message) and what he or she sees in your facial gestures (non-verbal message) must match. If they don't, guess which message carries the most weight? Right - the non-verbal message. You have probably heard all your life that what you do is much more believable than what you say. But nowhere is this more true than in one-to-one communication. In studies conducted with individuals who were sent mixed messages – ie., where the non-verbal did not match the verbal – they were influenced 93 per cent by non-verbal messages, and only 7 per cent by verbal messages.

Non-verbal messages

Non-verbal messages can be lumped together into several major categories: eye contact, posture, facial expressions and gestures, and the quality of your voice. Let's look briefly at each of these.

Eye contact

Why do some people speak the truth and yet look dishonest? Why can rascals lie and yet look absolutely believable? The answer is in their eyes!

Eyes are indeed the window of the soul. The soft gaze of the lover for his or her mate; the intense look that commands obedience; the eyes that smile at you as you talk; piercing, angry eyes – eyes are keys to your communication. And what your eyes communicate to others depends on:

1. how long you look;
2. where you look as you talk and listen; and
3. how long you blink your eyes.

How long you look. There is a big difference between staring eyes and darting eyes. The longer you look at a colleague without looking away, the more you may be seen as intimidating. But if your eyes dart away from the other person and then back again, you could be seen as shifty. The common factor is time. In conversations with colleagues, normal eye contact is somewhere between 5 and 10 seconds. A shorter look may cause you to appear sneaky to the other person. A longer look can result in the other person feeling threatened and uncomfortable.

Where you look as you talk and listen. If you look at the floor, walls, or ceiling as you communicate, you may appear to be disinterested in the conversation. If looking directly into someone's eyes makes you feel uncomfortable, try looking at some other part of the face. If you look at the other person's nose, chin or forehead, you will still appear to be looking into his or her eyes.

How long you blink your eyes. Blinking your eyes is normal. But some people slowly shut their eyes as they talk or listen. This gives the impression that they are removing themselves from the conversation with the other person.

Posture

Notice your posture the next time you are in a one-to-one conversation. If you are standing, do you have your weight evenly balanced on both feet and are you leaning slightly forward? Or are you resting your weight on one leg and leaning away? If seated, are you leaning towards or away from the other person?

Of course, most people have privacy zones. Lovers, little children, and intimate friends are usually allowed closer than colleagues. If you stand too close or lean too far forward, they may feel uncomfortable. In this country, a distance of less than 18 inches is considered intimate. Private conversations with close friends usually take place from 18 to 24 inches, normal conversations with colleagues are usually 2 to 4 feet, and business conversations often take place at a distance of 4 to 7 feet.

You can tell a lot about a relationship by observing how close people are to each other as they talk. For example, notice the difference in distance between you and your close friends compared to the distance between you and your boss. If your boss conducts participative performance appraisal reviews with you, he or she is likely to sit across the corner of his or her desk (2 to 4 feet). But if your boss is less participative in his or her management style, normal communication distance will usually be from 4 to 7 feet – ie., across the desk rather than across the corner of the desk.

Facial expressions and gestures

There are a number of different facial expressions and gestures that can communicate, including smiling, frowning, yawning, and using the hands.

The smile. A genuine smile is a wonderful thing. It implies acceptance, caring and friendship. When people are asked to place themselves into one of these three categories – seldom smiles, neutral expression or often smiles – the majority select 'often smiles'. But when people are asked to rate others using the same scale, the average falls between 'seldom smiles' and 'neutral'. So something strange is going on. People obviously think they smile more than they really do.

The danger is that you may also think you smile often – but don't. If you are smiling on the inside but others see a neutral expression, then you are not communicating what you are really feeling. On the other hand, if you are angry but are smiling, others will still get a mixed message. Your goal is to match what you say with what others see and with what you feel.

Frowning. A frown can communicate that you do not approve of what is being said, that you do not approve of the person with whom you are communicating, or that the situation you are in is disagreeable. Part of the problem is that the person you are talking to may not be able to tell if you are frowning because of the message, because of him or herself, or because of the situation. For example, I often frown when I am writing. It isn't that I'm unhappy with what I am doing or even unhappy with others who may be around me – I am simply concentrating. Because a frown, like a smile, is often unconscious, you need to know when you frown so that others will see a message that matches what you say.

Using the hands. I use my hands when I talk. For example, when I listen to someone talk and do not intend to interrupt, I will rest my chin on my hand. Or if I want to let the other person know that I need to say something, I will often slightly raise my hand – almost an abbreviated version of a classroom response. If I want to demonstrate caring to another, I may touch him or her lightly on the arm or shoulder. I may even use my fingers to emphasise a point, as in, 'There are three (holding up three fingers) areas to consider in looking at communication. First, (holding up my first finger) is the sender, second (holding up another finger) the message, and third (holding up three fingers) the receiver.' But I try very hard not to point my finger at another as I talk, because this may appear parental. And I also try not to tap my finger or a pencil on the desk as I am talking, because the other person may feel that I don't have time for him or her.

Quality of your voice

The two major factors that affect the quality of your voice are tone and pace. Your tone is a function of voice frequency, resonance and loudness. Pace is related to the speed at which you talk as well as your use of pauses.

Voice tone. Without training, it is difficult to change the resonance of your voice. But you can change the frequency and loudness of your normal speaking voice. It is possible, with practice, to change your natural frequency either up or down. If you feel that your voice is pitched too high, you can deliberately lower the frequency. Or if it is too low, you can raise it. If you speak too loudly or softly, you can also develop the habit of speaking at a more appropriate level.

Pace. This is the one that gets me into trouble. I'm all right until I get excited - then I talk too fast. Like most things, it is a habit. But over the years, I have been fairly successful in slowing down even when my mind is racing.

Pausing appropriately can also enhance the quality of your speech. Not only does it give you a chance to think more about what you are going to say, it also makes it easier for your listener to understand what you are saying. But it is also possible to overdo the pause. In this country, if you pause too long, the other person will feel the need to speak. So you need to find a balance - pausing often enough to improve the quality of your speech and at the same time not pausing so long that the other person begins to feel uncomfortable.

Verbal messages

By verbal, I mean the words that you use, the meaning that others give to your words, speech habits, and the use of questions. Let's look at each of these.

Jargon, technical language, abbreviations or acronyms

When words are unfamiliar to your receiver, or abstract in their meaning, then the probability of a communication problem is increased. When jargon, technical language, abbreviations, or acronyms (letters selected to represent a compound word or a series of words - eg., 'TNT' is an acronym from Trinitrotoluene) are used with others who are not familiar with them, the communication is much more difficult. In my field, for example, everybody knows what an 'HRD' specialist is. But since most of my readers are not 'HRD' specialists, I did not use HRD earlier, but spelled it out as human resource development.

There is nothing inherently wrong with jargon, technical language, abbreviations or acronyms - they can save time and help you to communicate more precisely with others who are in the same job or profession. But the use of jargon or over-technical language with people who don't have the foggiest idea what you're talking about is definitely poor communication.

The meaning of words

Words don't have meanings. People assign meaning to words. Meanings are assigned based on your own experience. If your experiences are different from mine, then it is likely that your meanings may also be different. For example, in this chapter I have used the word 'value' 13 times. Yet any dictionary will give a variety of definitions such as:

1. The worth of something in money
2. The purchasing power of sterling
3. What you desire or hold important in life
4. What society sees as important
5. The worth of a particular playing card.

When I used the word 'value' in the original rough draft of this chapter, I did not define it. Later, in editing it, one of the reviewers wrote, 'I have some concern that your readers will not clearly understand what you mean by "values".' So in the rewrite, I defined the word by saying, 'Values are those beliefs that are personally important to you in life.' Note, too, that I didn't just write the word 'acronym' in the beginning of this section, but also defined it as 'letters selected to represent a compound word or a series of words'.

Speech habits

There are people who end nearly every sentence with, 'OK?', 'Right', or 'You know?' Or they start every sentence with 'Well . . .' If you have a speech habit like any of these, be aware of the fact that it drives some people crazy. Your listeners can become so conscious of your use of a particular word that they will stop hearing what you're saying.

At this point, you have seen how communication can be affected by the sender's and the receiver's values and past experiences, their present viewpoints as a result of projections and attitudes, and the non-verbal and verbal parts of the message. The last step is to look at the feedback that the sender gets from the receiver, or vice versa.

Feedback

Feedback occurs not only when you stop talking and begin to listen to another; it also happens as you talk. You are certainly aware of the other person's expressions, for example, frowns or smiles - as well as other non-verbal gestures like nodding. These signals can tell you when your message is being received and even to some extent, if you are being understood.

But for the most part, communication without verbal feedback is nothing more than a presentation. If you really want to talk to rather than at someone, then you've got to listen to what the other person has to say.

Non-verbal feedback

Listen without interrupting
This basic rule of communication and courtesy is often violated. In conversation, you may become so interested in what you want to say next, that you don't really listen to what other people are saying. Since you can speak at a rate of about 150 words per minute but can listen at well over 750, you are going to have a lot of extra time while someone else is talking. This is both a curse and a blessing. It's a curse because as someone else speaks, your thoughts are likely to be going in a dozen different directions. And if you follow through an interesting thought, you may lose track of what the other person is saying. But it's a blessing because the extra time can give you a chance to really concentrate on the other person, focusing on what he or she is saying, and trying to understand the message in the light of your own past experience.

Nodding
You can encourage verbal feedback by nodding as the other person talks. There was an interesting study that demonstrated that one nod increased the flow of communication, two nods neither increased nor decreased communication, and three or more nods in rapid succession decreased communication. These results do seem to fit with my experience. Single nods appropriately spaced certainly do encourage others to continue to talk. And I have known people who nodded so much and so often that it was distracting.

Posture

Your posture while listening to another person shows how attentive you are. You pay attention to the other person while talking or listening when your body communicates that you are interested in being with them. If you are standing, balance your weight on both feet and lean slightly forward. If you are seated just lean forward. This is attending.

Of course, there are individuals who will talk your ears off if you let them. With people like this, a well-timed interruption is appropriate. But really listening to what someone else is saying is beneficial, for several reasons. First, it will help you to gain more information; and in general, the more information you have, the better will be your response. Second, listening is very complimentary – we all like to be listened to! Finally, sometimes people don't want, or need, a response. They just want someone to listen.

Verbal feedback

There are a number of ways you can verbally encourage the other person to give you feedback. You can reflect on what someone is saying or feeling, you can ask questions and you can summarise.

Reflecting

To obtain more information or feedback, you can simply restate what the other person has said and ask if what you heard was correct. Or you can state the feelings that you saw in the other person and again ask if what you saw was correct. Either way works – by encouraging the other person to continue to talk.

For example, suppose that you and I were not only colleagues but shared the car-journey to and from work together. One day while having a break you said, 'Dick, maybe if your work area wasn't quite so untidy, it wouldn't take us so long to get out of here at the end of the day'. Somewhat irritated I replied, 'Well, if you weren't such a perfectionist and could live with a little more normal disorder in your life, it wouldn't be a problem!'

At this point, you have two ways of reflecting my statement. You could focus on the facts by saying, 'You see me as a perfectionist and think that your desk is normal, is that correct?' Then stay silent, and I will probably respond. On the other hand, you could reflect my feelings by saying, 'You seem irritated that I see your work area as untidy, is that right?' Again, keep your mouth closed and wait for my response.

Asking questions
Asking good questions is an excellent way of obtaining feedback from the other person. For example, if you made a comment about your job to a colleague and she responded by saying 'I really do hate my job!', you might respond by telling her all the things you, too, don't like about your job. But a better communication strategy would be to ask, 'What is it about the job that bothers you most?' Then, listen as she tells you!

Open questions. Note the use of an 'open' question – the one that began with the word 'What' – in the above example. Open questions begin with the words, 'What, How, When, Where, Who, Which or Why'. They are used to gain more information, and cannot usually be answered with just 'Yes' or 'No'.

Open questions that yield the most information usually start with 'What' or 'How'. Other open questions, beginning with 'When' or 'Where' can also help you to understand the other person, since they obtain more specific details; but they are also less useful for acquiring general information. The least desirable questions seem to be the personal 'Why' question – as in 'Why do you hate this job?' If your colleague is a good friend, this question is probably all right. But if not, a 'Why' combined with 'you' can produce defensive behaviour, since the question focuses on personal motives.

Closed questions. 'Closed' questions, on the other hand, are those used to direct or guide discussions – and are normally answered with a 'Yes' or 'No'. For example, 'Do you . . .?', 'Have you . . .?', 'Are you . . .?' 'Would you . . .?' 'Can you . . .?', and 'Should you . . .?' are closed questions. Some questions in this category are perceived as requests for more information; but technically they are 'closed' questions. For instance, questions like, 'Can you be more specific?' or 'Could you give me an example?' are not normally answered with 'Yes' or 'No', even though they are in fact closed questions. Thus they are good questions to use in obtaining feedback from the other person.

Guided questions. Another way to enhance communication is to use 'guided' questions. Guided questions direct the discussion to either the positive or negative side of an issue. For example, if your colleague responded to you by saying, 'I really like my job, but my family hates it,' you can guide the discussion to either side of this statement by asking:

'What do you like about your job?' (positive)
'How does your job affect your family?' (negative)

Loaded questions. When asking or answering questions, carefully avoid what are termed 'loaded' questions. Suppose you made a comment about your boss, Carol. Your colleague responds by saying, 'Don't you think Carol is a pain?' Your colleague did not really ask a 'question'. He or she actually stated an *opinion* in the form of a question. Questions like, 'Don't you think . . .?', 'Don't you feel . . .?', or 'Wouldn't you agree that . . .?' are really just expressions of the speaker's strong opinion. People often mask opinions as questions because they feel it is 'safer' than saying openly, 'I believe that . . .!' If you want to find out what someone else believes or feels, you should ask them directly. And if you have an opinion about something that you want to express, then you should be equally direct and express that opinion without putting it in the form of a 'loaded' question.

Summarising

Summarising what you heard the other person say is a powerful communication tool for the following reasons:

1. It will help to ensure that what you heard is what the other person really said.
2. It will force you to listen better.
3. It will improve your retention.
4. If you keep quiet after your summary, the other person will probably give you additional information.

You don't need a tape recorder to summarise what the other person said. Just listen intently, and when the other person is finished speaking, simply summarise what you have heard.

As we have seen, one-to-one communication is not simple at all – it is quite complex. I hope that you have gained additional insight into the process of communication by reading about the sender and receiver, the message, and the need to obtain feedback about what was said. The following pages are designed to help you put into practice the concepts presented in this chapter.

Communication analysis
Part 1

This work sheet is designed to help you develop your communication skills. It will show you how to plan a communication session with another person and will help you in self-assessment afterwards.

If additional work sheets are needed, please copy these pages.

Name of person you will be interviewing: ____________________

1. Consider your similarities and differences in background

Indicate sex: You ___________ The other person _______

Age:
Big difference __ Somewhat different __ No difference __

Education:
Big difference __ Somewhat different __ No difference __

Income:
Big difference __ Somewhat different __ No difference __

Race: Different _________ Same _________

How might differences get in the way of my communication with this other person?

____

____

____

2. Possible projections

What, if anything, don't I like about this person that I also don't like in myself? ______________________________

____

____

Could this be a projection of my own imagination on to the other person, or is he or she really this way? ____________

What, if anything, irritates or concerns me about this person that might get in the way of our communication? __________

____

Again, could this be a projection of my own feelings? ________

3. Attitudes

What problems have I had in the past with this person that influence my feelings towards him or her? ________________
____
____

What can I do about any unresolved problems that may exist?
____
____

What, if any, 'games' do we play? (eg, 'Nothing', 'Kidding around', 'The agreeables', or 'Dancing').
____
____

After completing this section of your communication analysis, arrange a private interview with this person to discuss your answers and resolve any differences in opinions if possible.

Communication analysis
Part 2

When you have finished discussing Part 1, ask the other person to give you honest feedback on the following questions.

1. Non-verbal messages

Eye contact

- My length of eye contact is:
  Too long ________ Just right ________ Too short ________
- Where do I look when I talk to you? ____________________
  ____
- Do I shut my eyes too long when I communicate with you? __

Facial expressions and gestures

- How often do I smile?
  Not enough ______ Enough ______ Too much ______

- How often do I frown?
  Not enough ______ Enough ______ Too much ______
- How much do I use my hands when I talk?
  Enough ______________ Not enough ______________

  If not enough, how could I improve? ______________________
  ____
  ____
  ____

2. Verbal messages

Quality of my voice

- How is the pitch (frequency) of my voice?
  Too low ________ Just right ________ Too high ________
- How is the loudness of my voice?
  Too soft ______ Just right ______ Too loud ______
- Do I pause appropriately? Yes ______ No ______
- How well do I balance the time I talk with the time I listen?
  Don't talk enough ______ Good balance ______ Talk too much ________

Jargon, technical language, abbreviations or acronyms

- Do I use jargon, technical language, abbreviations or acronyms when I communicate? Yes ________ No ________

  If so, what kind of problems does this cause in my communication? ______________________________________
  ____
  ____
  ____

- How well do I use words to communicate?
  Need improvement __________ OK __________
  If my vocabulary needs improving, how should I improve it?
  ____
  ____
  ____

- Do I have any speech habits that interfere with communication?
  No __________ Yes __________ If so, what? __________
  ____
  ____

3. Feedback

Non-verbal feedback

- How often do you feel that I interrupt you when we are talking?
  Seldom __________ Often __________
- Do I nod my head appropriately as I listen to you?
  Seldom ______ OK ______ Too much nodding ______
- How would you judge my posture? In other words, do I look as though I am really listening to you as you talk? ________
  ____
  ____
  ____
  ____

Verbal feedback

- How well do I reflect to you what I thought I heard you say?
  ____
  ____
  ____
  ____
- How well do I use questions to find out more about how you feel about the topic under discussion? ________________
  ____
  ____
  ____
  ____
- How well do I summarise what you have said in a conversation?
  ____
  ____
  ____
  ____
  ____

When the interview is over, consider in private the conversation you had. Note below the key points your learned about yourself.

As a result of what you have learned, what are you going to do to improve your communication skills further?

Chapter 4

Working Effectively with Others

If you stop to consider people you would enjoy working with, it's often fairly easy to think of some names. It is also easy to think of people you would definitely *not* want to work with! But did you ever wonder why? Why do some people seem desirable as work partners and other appear undesirable?

Consider those individuals you would enjoy working with by thinking of short 'descriptions' of them. Words and phrases may quickly spring to mind – such as:

Friendly	Does his or her share and more
Doesn't take all the credit	Hard working
Loyal	Does what he says he's going to do
Doesn't complain	Has good work habits
Not bossy	Talks to me
Easygoing	Serious about his or her job
Honest with me and others	Doesn't get sidetracked
Has good ideas	Helpful
Not critical	

Sometimes what seems like a strength can also cause trouble. For example, someone could see us as non-critical (a strength). But this characteristic might cause us to have difficulty giving constructive feedback to an individual when it is justified, and even desired. Or the strength 'talks to me' can cause a problem if the individual talks too much. In fact, we can create a continuum concerning almost any of the descriptions above. For example:

×	×	×
Silent and withdrawn	Talks appropriately	Talks too much

The secret of working with people is to avoid the extremes. But unfortunately, we don't always know where we are on the continuum, probably because we don't see ourselves as clearly as others do.

Two psychologists, Joseph Luft and Harry Ingham, developed a model that can help us to understand ourselves better. Their model, called the 'Johari Window', looks like an old-fashioned window with four panes of glass.

1. What I know about me. What others know about me.	2. What I know about me. What others don't know about me.
3. What I don't know about me. What others know about me.	4. What I don't know about me. What others don't know about me.

Block 1 contains all those things that I am aware of, and that others also know. For example, I am very much aware that I can't spell, and my colleagues also know this about me.

Block 2 contains those aspects that I am aware of but don't choose to tell anyone else. An example of this happened in a class I was once enrolled in. Our instructor told a joke that clearly demonstrated his prejudice against black people. His assumption was that we were all of one mind and would find his so-called joke funny. It wasn't funny to me. In fact, I was offended that he thought that I would find it humorous. At that moment, I was very much aware of my feelings – he was not.

Suppose we consider my instructor the subject 'I' in the Johari Window illustration. Unaware of his impact on others (me, in this case) he would be in Block 3. That is, he knew that he used ethnic humour, but wasn't aware of its impact on others.

At the end of the class, I asked him if he would like some private feedback. When he said yes, I told him how I felt about the 'joke'. It was to his credit that he accepted the feedback graciously and changed his behaviour in the future. By being open to feedback, he moved from Block 3 to Block 1, thus increasing his self-knowledge.

People are reluctant to give others feedback because they are afraid of hurting their feelings. But without feedback, how can we learn about those things that others see, but we don't?

Part of the answer is to find a way to ask others for feedback. One way is to copy the following pages describing how others see you and then ask some trusted friends to fill them in. While you are waiting for their responses, fill in the same pages in terms of how you see yourself. Then compare how your friends saw you with how you saw yourself.

You may find it easier to ask several people to complete this form anonymously. Friends may feel more comfortable and be more truthful if asked to fill in the survey anonymously.

After receiving and recording the completed reviews from your friends, look carefully at their ratings. Then compare their ratings with your own self-assessment. Note areas where your raters do not perceive you as you view yourself. Realising that others see you differently from the way you see yourself and examining why, is an important step in understanding yourself better and improving your way of relating.

Finally – and most importantly – note those ratings that are less than 2 (ie., 0 and 1 ratings). These ratings (on either side of 5) indicate the extremes of positive traits, and might suggest areas that need improvement in your relationship with that person on the job.

If you have areas where your own self-perception differs greatly from your raters' view, or areas where your ratings are less than 2 (suggesting imbalances), arrange to meet privately with your raters to discuss these areas. Even if your survey was conducted anonymously, you can still conduct follow-up interviews and ask your friends if they concur with the feedback. If so, ask them for specific examples of why they perceive you as they do in these areas. Then you will be in a position to decide whether you need to change your style of working, and working with others.

As an example of this process, imagine that several of my friends give me less than 2 in the category of 'Hard working', as too hard working. My first task is to talk to each of them and ask for examples of their perception. Then I am in a better position to make decisions about whether or not I want to change. I may decide that I like being seen as 'working too hard'. But the fact that I 'work too hard' may also cause problems for others. For

Working effectively with others

Name of the person being reviewed ________________

Name of the person filling in this form ________________

Date ________________

By putting an X in the appropriate box, please indicate below your opinion of me in each of the17 areas. I've asked you to complete this review because you are my friend. True friends give honest feedback. Therefore, be as honest as possible in your review.

In my work with others, how do you rate me on the following:

1. Friendliness

0	1	2	3	4	5	4	3	2	1	0

Unfriendly — Friendly — Excessively friendly

2. Giving credit for work done with others

0	1	2	3	4	5	4	3	2	1	0

Takes all the credit — Gives credit when due — Cannot take credit

3. Loyalty

0	1	2	3	4	5	4	3	2	1	0

Disloyal — Loyal — Blindly supportive

4. Expressing complaints

0	1	2	3	4	5	4	3	2	1	0

Constantly complains — Complains when justified — Never complains

5. Ability to lead

0	1	2	3	4	5	4	3	2	1	0

Bossy — Takes lead when called for — Never assumes leadership

6. Honesty and integrity

0	1	2	3	4	5	4	3	2	1	0

Dishonest — Honest — Rigidly honest (wears a halo)

7. Suggesting good ideas about the job

0	1	2	3	4	5	4	3	2	1	0

Seldom offers ideas — Offers helpful ideas — Offers too many ideas

8. Constructively critical

0	1	2	3	4	5	4	3	2	1	0

Critical of everything — Gives criticism constructively — Never gives constructive feedback

9. Doing one's share

0	1	2	3	4	5	4	3	2	1	0

Always tries to get someone else to do the work — Does share — Tries to do everyone's work

10. Hard working

0	1	2	3	4	5	4	3	2	1	0

Lazy — Makes a good effort — Works too hard

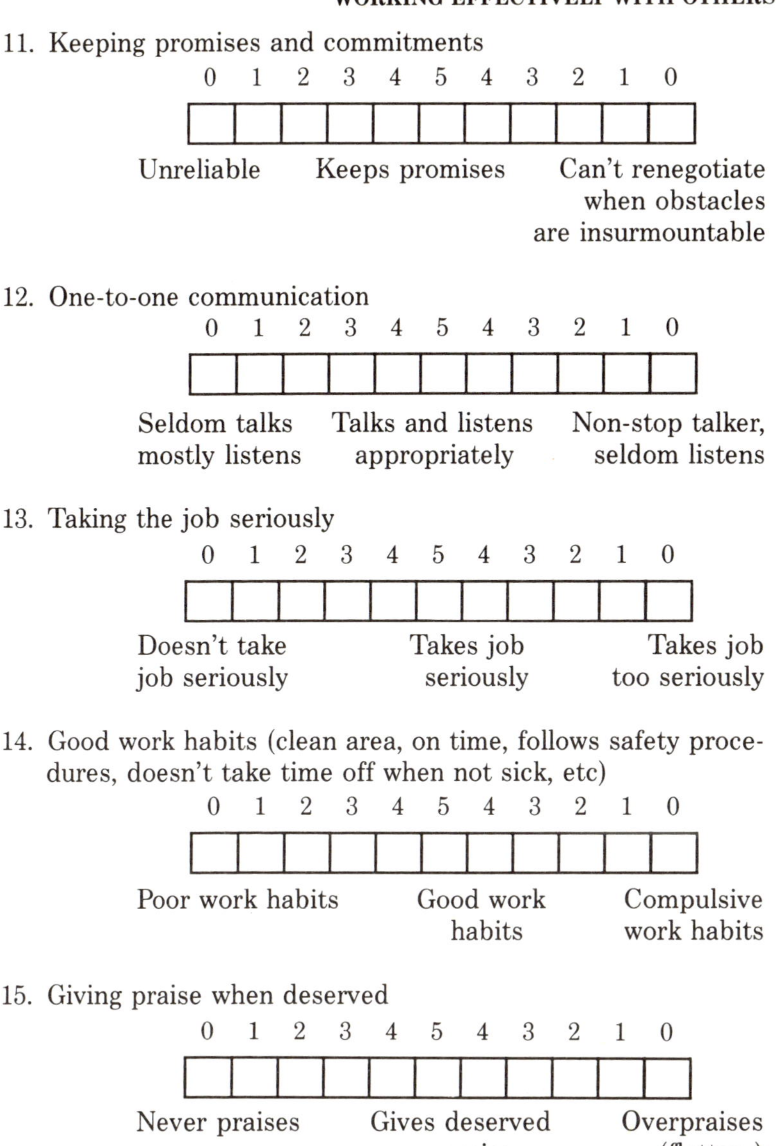

11. Keeping promises and commitments

0	1	2	3	4	5	4	3	2	1	0

Unreliable — Keeps promises — Can't renegotiate when obstacles are insurmountable

12. One-to-one communication

0	1	2	3	4	5	4	3	2	1	0

Seldom talks mostly listens — Talks and listens appropriately — Non-stop talker, seldom listens

13. Taking the job seriously

0	1	2	3	4	5	4	3	2	1	0

Doesn't take job seriously — Takes job seriously — Takes job too seriously

14. Good work habits (clean area, on time, follows safety procedures, doesn't take time off when not sick, etc)

0	1	2	3	4	5	4	3	2	1	0

Poor work habits — Good work habits — Compulsive work habits

15. Giving praise when deserved

0	1	2	3	4	5	4	3	2	1	0

Never praises — Gives deserved praise — Overpraises (flattery)

16. Helpfulness

0	1	2	3	4	5	4	3	2	1	0

Never helps — Helps others appropriately — Tries to be too helpful

After completing the evaluation, record the scores for each description below:

	Friend A	Friend B	Friend C	Friend D	Your self-rating
1. Friendliness	____	____	____	____	____
2. Giving credit for work done	____	____	____	____	____
3. Loyalty	____	____	____	____	____
4. Expressing complaints when appropriate	____	____	____	____	____
5. Ability to lead	____	____	____	____	____
6. Honesty	____	____	____	____	____
7. Suggesting good ideas about the job	____	____	____	____	____
8. Constructively critical	____	____	____	____	____
9. Doing one's share	____	____	____	____	____
10. Hard working	____	____	____	____	____
11. Keeping promises and commitments	____	____	____	____	____
12. One-to-one communication	____	____	____	____	____
13. Taking the job seriously	____	____	____	____	____
14. Good working habits	____	____	____	____	____
15. Giving praise when deserved	____	____	____	____	____
16. Helpfulness	____	____	____	____	____
Subtotals	____	____	____	____	____

Total points (A + B + C + D) ____

Average number of points (Total points divided by number of reviewers ____ example others who must process my work may begin to feel overloaded with my output.

If you decide that you need to do something about a specific area, the next step is to develop a plan for change. Here again, your friends can help in providing ideas to include in your plan.

And one word of caution: don't overwhelm yourself trying to change in too many areas at once. There is plenty of time to make important changes in your way of relating to others and the job. Simply ask yourself, 'What are the three most important things I want to change today?' - and do it consistently!

Change may not be easy. But it is possible! It first takes a clear understanding of what needs to be changed, then a willingness to do so. But it is also nice to have support while you are making important and significant changes. So if you have a close friend, spouse, or confidant, you may wish to ask him or her to help see you through each stage of your change. One thing is certain - the results will be very rewarding to you and others!

On the next page is an interview and planning form which you can use to obtain additional information from your friends.

Working effectively with others
Interview form

1. Area(s) of improvement that I need to investigate:

____

____

____

2. Friend(s), or others, I want to interview.

____________________ ____________________

____________________ ____________________

____________________ ____________________

Interview(s)

3. Examples and/or illustrations of area(s) of concern:

____

____

____

____

____

____

4. Answers to the question, 'How does this have a negative impact on my performance or on our relationship?'

____

____

____

____

____

____

5. Ideas on what I can do about this situation if I decide that change is beneficial:

____

____

____

____

____

____

____

Chapter 5

How to Receive Work Assignments

Suppose your boss has just asked you to complete a task, but you don't have the foggiest idea how to do it. At this point you can:

1. Ask questions to find out more about the task.
2. Say, 'I don't know how to do that job.'
3. Say, 'That's not *my* job.'
4. Ignore the assignment.

Which of the four responses is the most responsible?

Number one – 'ask questions' is probably the best response. Number two is a passive response; and number three is hostile. Actually, responses two and three are very similar. They both communicate to the boss that you don't want to do the job. And answer number four is a potential disaster, not only for you, but also for your boss and colleagues. When assigned work is ignored, it can cause serious hardship for others who depend on you.

A key step in becoming an effective employee is to accept responsibility. Success starts with you! If you are assigned a task that you don't know how to do, ask questions. 'What exactly do you want me to do?' 'Where can I go to find out how it ought to be done?' 'How do you want me to proceed?' 'Is there a specific sequence that would be more efficient in completing this task?'

For more complicated assignments, ask your supervisor to help you write out a step-by-step procedure. Start by asking what the end result of the task should look like. Then ask your boss if he or she has any preference as to how the task can best be accomplished. Take notes and then read them back to your supervisor to help ensure understanding of the assignment. During this part of the discussion, you can also offer ideas on how to improve the quality of the job. These comments will communicate to your supervisor that you understand what is being discussed.

The amount of information you need depends a lot on what you already know about the assigned task – and your boss's delegation style. The more you already know about the task, the fewer questions you may need to ask. If your boss has a delegation style that encourages you to take responsibility for the details of the plan, you may choose to ask only questions that define the general outline of the job, not the specific details. In this case, a better approach is to receive the assignment and determine any required deadlines, sketch out in private a general plan of attack, and then discuss the plan with your boss. If you're lucky enough to work for a supervisor who will allow you to take the initiative, then take it!

Another way of visualising a new task is to ask questions about how it may be compared with an old task. Also, you can ask for an example, illustration, or a demonstration.

Misunderstandings occur when both the supervisor and the employee think there is mutual understanding of what was said – and there wasn't. So don't be afraid to repeat your questions if you are not sure you understand what was said. And when you receive an answer to a question you can repeat, in your own words, what you thought you heard, and ask if that is correct. You will be amazed at the number of times your supervisor will say, 'No, not exactly. What I said was . . .'

You can even ask 'Why?' questions – tactfully. Even though the days of 'Because I said so!' are mostly gone, a why question can still sound challenging unless it is well-phrased. A simple 'Why is it important that this be done?' is usually less threatening to your supervisor than, 'Why do I have to do this?' If you can determine the reasons why something needs to be done, they will help you greatly in carrying out the task. 'Why' answers will often make it easier to understand the importance of the new task. They will also help you do the best thing, or make the right decisions, if things don't go exactly as planned.

It is also important for you to be aware what the final results of your work should be. In other words, what is a 'good' job? Or what should the job or task look like when you have finished it? These questions are important because (1) they allow you to measure your own performance; and (2) they will help you to know when you have completed the assignment.

You can also ask your supervisor when he or she will be available for additional questions. It can be very frustrating to be two hours into a new task and suddenly discover the need for additional information – only to find that your boss is out of the office for the rest of the afternoon.

The most important thing is to *ask questions*! Good questions are:

Questions to the Boss	**Questions to Myself**
'When do you want me to start?'	What am I now doing that may interfere with this new task?
'When should the job be completed?'	Are other activities already arranged that would interfere with the deadline?
'Where can I go to find out how it ought to be done?'	What don't I know that I need to know to complete this task?
'What potential problems do you see?'	What potential problems do I see?
'Which other people should I see about this?'	Who else is likely to be involved in this? Are they people that I can easily talk to?
'How often do you want feedback on my progress?	How hard is it going to be for me to tell the boss if things don't go well? If I find that I need to do things a little differently, how much does the boss need to know? How approachable is my boss?
'What does good performance on this job look like?'	How will I know when I've done a good job? What is going to happen if I don't do this properly?

These questions appear on a check sheet found on the next page. This page can be reproduced by you and used to help you in receiving work assignments.

How to receive work assignments
Check sheet

1. Why is it important that this be done?

____

____

____

2. When do you want me to begin? ____________________

3. When should the job be completed? ________________

4. Where can I go to find out how it ought to be done?

____

____

____

5. What potential problems do you see?

____

____

____

6. What potential problems do I see?

____

____

____

7. Who else should I see? ________________________

8. How often do you want feedback on my progress?

____

____

____

9. What does a 'good' job look like?

____

____

____

10. When will you be available if I have additional questions? Whom should I consult if you are unavailable?

____

Chapter 6

How to Solve Problems

Some people seem to have a knack for coming up with the best solution to a problem. Others with the same intelligence and experience seem to come up with solutions before they are even sure what the problems are! We've all seen examples of disasters that occurred when the cause of the problem wasn't accurately pinpointed before expensive action was taken: decisions that resulted in wasted time, materials and money; plans that looked perfect on paper, but failed in real life.

This chapter will help you to develop skills in problem-solving. It will show you logical – and simple – ways to make your problem-solving effective.

A key step emphasised in this chapter is writing out the problem. It is amazing what a simple thing like writing down information can do to increase your success in solving problems. You don't always have a clipboard in your hand, but, whenever you have a problem, begin by taking a minute to make the problem 'visible' in writing.

Visibility does several things:

- First, if a problem-solving process is taking place only in your mind, no one can help you. Others are kept from pointing out oversights, errors or faulty assumptions.
- Second, if you do not make your thinking visible, you do not have a reliable way to review how you attempted to solve a problem and therefore to learn from your past mistakes.
- Third, writing the problem down will help you to see the whole problem, rather than just disorganised bits and pieces.

Situation analysis

'Situation analysis' (SA) is a problem-solving tool that will help you to break a large, even messy, situation down into manageable pieces. These pieces become the problems, decisions, plans or even the new problem situations to be analysed. So when you have a problem that is big, complex, bulky and has lots of bits and pieces, this is probably the time for SA. Problems like 'I'm unhappy at work', 'I don't get on with my boss', or 'I have trouble at home' are often called problems. Technically, they are not problems at all, but statements about symptoms of problems. And for concerns like these, a good tool to reach for is situation analysis.

Let's take a messy situation, and see how SA can be used to break it down.

The case of the unhappy employee

> My name is Phil. I am employed by the British Data Corporation whose headquarters are in London. I'm married, have two children, a fairly large dog (Golden Retriever), and a cat of unknown origin that was left on our doorstep a couple of years ago. I drive about 30 miles to work (it takes me about 90 minutes), and so I spend about an hour and a half in the car every day. The traffic is getting worse. More cars, lorries and buses! Sometimes I wonder if the world will end up as one huge car park.
>
> Speaking of parking – what a pain! If I park in the street, my car gets towed away, or I get a parking ticket, or I lose my hubcaps. Two weeks ago my car got towed away, I got a parking ticket, *and* two of my hubcaps were stolen. Lately, I've been keeping my car in a multi-storey car park. The cost is horrendous (but hubcaps are even more expensive; I paid £30 plus VAT for the two hubcaps!).
>
> My company has just introduced a new medical scheme. They used to pay 100 per cent of the cost. It covered glasses, dental work and visits to our private family doctor. This new scheme not only restricts us to their list of approved doctors (our doctor is not on the list); I now have to pay half of the monthly premium.
>
> My boss is having serious trouble with her marriage. I know how difficult this must be for her, but I wish she could leave her problem at home. I know she can't, but I still wish she would. She's irritable and withdrawn, so it's really hard to be around her. It's been months since she has given anybody a pat on the back. She is so wrapped up in her own problems that she doesn't have time for us any more. In fact, it seems to me that she resents it when we do need her for something.

But what bothers me most is that I was passed over for promotion. I was given some story about how the other person was better qualified. I don' t believe it. I know the other person and she is not better qualified. The only reason she got promoted instead of me is that she's a 'she'! I know that our Equal Opportunities ratios are in trouble. But why are they penalising me for what they did years ago? It just isn't fair. With all the expenses I have, I could really do with the extra money.

Money is tight. I took Gladys (our dog, not my wife) to the vet recently with a skin rash. Have you paid a vet's bill lately? £15! And Betty, my wife, wants to give up her job and find part-time employment so she can go back to university. That's good – but how are we going to pay for it?

My car just completed 100,000 miles. It was fun watching all those noughts come up. But what isn't fun is that the water pump needs replacing – again! This will be the third time that I've replaced the water pump on that car. And talk about money. It used to be that if you spent £75 in a garage, you had something substantial done. Now, £75 just about pays for a replacement water pump!

I have this dream. One morning, I drive to work, but I don't stop. I slide on to the M4 and head west. The sun is at my back, and the open road is ahead. I'm free. No worries, no responsibilities! I stop for lunch in Shrewsbury, have supper in Betws-y-coed, and watch the sun set over the Irish Sea. Then I take the car ferry to Dun Laoghaire – and drive up into the Wicklow Mountains. I'm usually a fairly optimistic individual. But things are not going well. Maybe what I need is to start looking for another job. I've been with the company 11 years – but I don't think I can put up with much more.

1. Write down the problem

The first step in using situation analysis is to make the problem statement visible. *Write it down!*

2. Separate the problem into its related parts

Separating out the pieces allows you to focus your energy on those areas that most affect the initial problem – and at the same time to see the problem as a whole. At this point, you don't have to analyse or conclude anything. Just jot down as many bits and pieces of the problem as you can think of. In our example, Phil would ask himself the question: 'What are the things that make me say, "I'm unhappy"?'

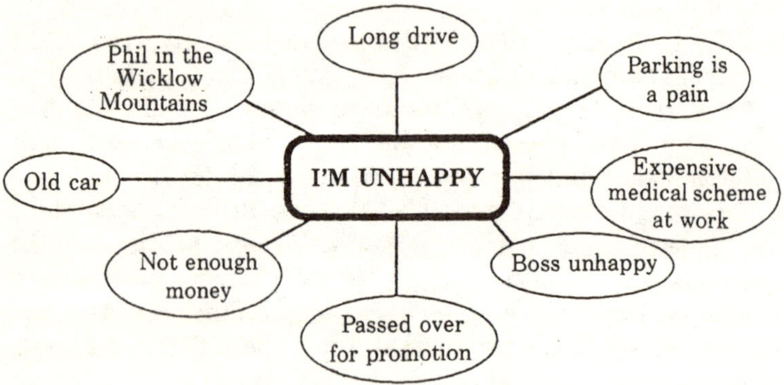

3. Determine which pieces are probable causes and which are probable results

In this step, decide which of the separate pieces are causes, and which are *results* of causes. To fix a mess you must attack the causes, not the results. This is why your first step is to determine the probable causes.

Indicate a probable cause by drawing an arrow pointing to the problem situation, and a problem result with an arrow pointing away from the problem. Then cross out the results, and focus your energies on the causes. Here's an example:

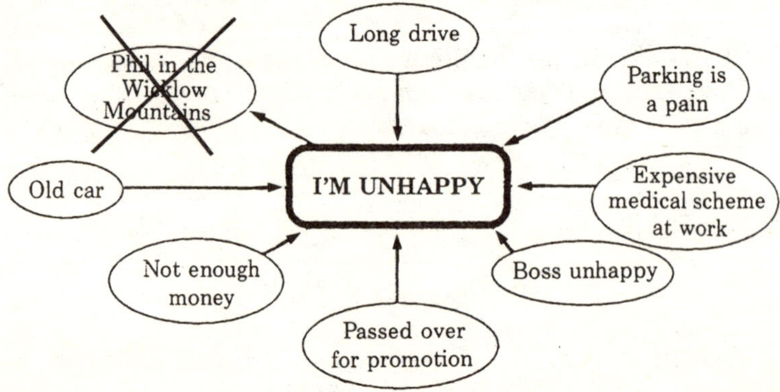

Phil's fantasies are a result of his present unhappiness. They are also causing his unhappiness to intensify (his dreams feel so good that they make his real world feel worse). If a piece of the situation seems to be both a probable cause *and* result treat it as a probable cause. In this case, the likelihood is that Phil's fantasies are a result of his unhappiness. They should be crossed out.

4. Set priorities

Many problems have a number of related causes, some major and some minor. To be effective, you need to devote your time to the major areas that can be changed. With tight schedules, you just don't have time to do everything. Therefore, fix the things that matter most by making them visible components, determining causes and results, and then assigning priorities only to the causes, not the results.

A simple way to assign priorities is to use the categories of 'Seriousness', 'Urgency' and 'Growth'. Rate each suspected cause with reference to these three categories in terms of high, medium, or low. To do this, ask the following types of question concerning each cause:

Seriousness: How serious is this cause in relation to the other causes?
How big is it?
How bad is it?
How frequently is it occurring?
Moneywise, how important is this piece of the problem?

Urgency: Do I have to drop everything else and take care of this today?
Can I do it just as well next week?
Can this part of the problem wait until next month?

Growth: If I don't take care of it now, will it get worse?
Will it soon spread out of control?

Phil finds that he can now analyse his problem fairly easily by using the 'Seriousness/Urgency/Growth' (SUG) system to rate each cause H (high), M (medium) or L (low). It seems to work best to rate the 'Seriousness' of each cause first, next rate 'Urgency' and last rate 'Growth'.

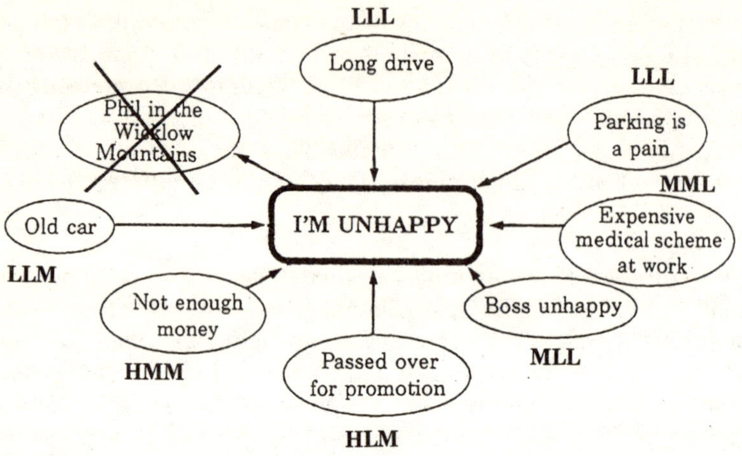

At this point, note that Phil rated two parts of his problem as 'high' in seriousness: 'Not enough money', and 'Passed over for promotion'. But his urgency rating was M for 'Not enough money', and L in 'Passed over for promotion'. You may feel that if the seriousness of a problem is high, then the urgency must be high, and the growth factor must also be high. Be careful not to allow a high seriousness rating to influence your ratings of urgency and growth. In Phil's case, 'Not enough money' was serious to him. But he felt that the urgency of this cause was only M and that the growth factor was also only M.

Similarly, even though he rated 'Passed over for promotion' as high in seriousness, he rated it low in urgency. Phil needs to do something about this piece of the problem. But realistically, it is not something that must be taken care of today – or even this week. In fact, it might be better if he would give this cause some time and solid thought before doing anything about it. Phil wisely rated this piece of the problem as low in growth. Yes, the problem is bad; but, no, the problem is not likely to get any worse. It is probably as bad as it is ever going to be right now. Therefore, it has low growth potential.

5. Decide which of the causes are: problems, decisions, plans, or new messes

The final step in situation analysis is to label each of the major causes of the situation as follows:

Problems to be diagnosed. For example, 'Passed over for promotion' may be a very real problem because Phil doesn't really know what the cause is. He thinks it is an equal opportunities situation; but that is only an assumption at this point. He needs to learn why he was passed over for promotion. Only when he finds out why this occurred is he ready to take some kind of action to address this problem.

Decisions that must be made. For example, Phil's new medical scheme will require his family to make some decisions about their future coverage.

Plans to be implemented. For example, Phil knows why the car requires a lot of maintenance (100,000 miles). And he knows what he wants to do about it (buy a new car). But buying a new car will require careful planning in order to make it happen.

New messes (new situations that must be further broken down). For example, 'Not enough money' may be a new situation to be analysed, with its own set of causes and results.

Here is Phil's labelling of his problem causes as either problems, decisions, plans, or new messes.

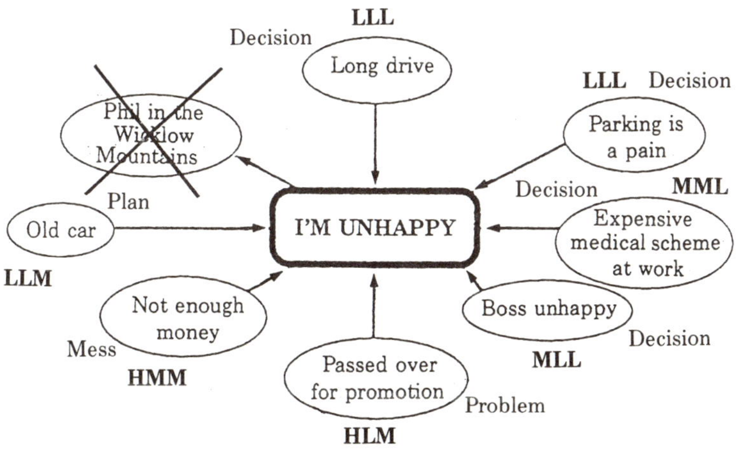

After you have analysed the parts of your problem by using situation analysis, you are ready to spend your time on the high priority causes. SA will not hand you some predetermined solution to your problem, but it does help you to make the various parts of your problem visible. Evaluate each part in a meaningful way, and decide where to focus your energy.

Each priority part of the situation analysis can then be looked at as an opportunity – an opportunity to do something differently and better.

You can use the work sheet below for analysing your problem situations.

Situation analysis
Work sheet

1. Write down the problem.

2. Separate the problem into its related parts.

3. Determine which pieces are probable causes and which are results.

4. Set SUG priorities, H = high, M = medium, L = low, on the causes.

   Seriousness — How bad? How big? How much money?
   Urgency — Do we have to take care of it today? Will next week be just as good?
   Growth — Is it getting worse? Or is it as bad as it is going to get?

5. Label the major causes: 'Problems'; 'Decision'; 'Plan'; new 'Mess'.

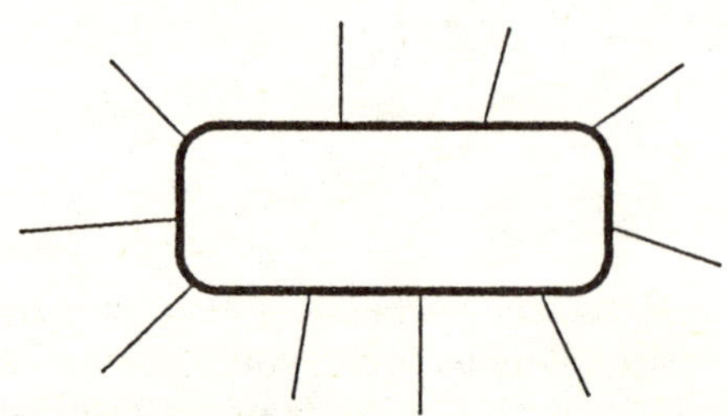

Finding causes

When trying to remedy a problem, many people jump into action without thinking. They just can't seem to help it: they want to be 'doing' something – anything. In fact, taking action without thinking, no matter how unproductive, can become a way of life. Before – repeat, *before* – you take action to solve a problem, look for causes. When you find the causes, fix the cause that is most clearly connected to the problem.

When you problem solve, you are finding the cause of a problem – not analysing a situation, making a decision, or implementing a plan. You are problem solving when:

1. *You have a deviation from the standard.*
   Something should be happening, but it isn't. It was supposed to have happened, but it didn't. It wasn't supposed to happen, but it did. All of these are deviations from standard.

2. *You find that the cause is uncertain.*
   If you already know the cause, then your next step is to make a decision by selecting the best way to remedy the problem.

3. *You are concerned.*
   If you see a deviation from standard, and you don't know why it happened but you are not concerned about it – you have no problem.

You can find the cause of a problem by following these seven steps:

1. *Make a written problem statement.*
   In writing out your problem statement, make it specific and negative. Write 'Passed over for promotion to supervisor', not just 'Lost promotion'. This not only helps to pinpoint the problem, but also highlights what the real issue is.

2. *Ask what, where, and when the problem is occurring: and what, where, and when the problem is not occurring.*
   At times causes can be located more quickly if you clarify what is not the problem as well as what is. The better you define the boundaries of a problem by specifying what the

problem is not, the better you can determine the most probable causes.

Also in Step 2 you ask, 'What is the extent of the problem?' In other words, how bad or serious is the problem? This information can keep you from developing a £500 solution to fix a £5 problem.

These What?/Where?/When?/Extent? questions help you to locate and isolate the problem area, and show you where to look for causes. An electronics technician calls it 'troubleshooting'; a doctor calls is 'diagnosing'. You might say it is 'working smarter, not harder'.

For example, suppose you have a bad pain. Now, what kind of questions would your doctor ask before he says, 'Take two aspirins and call me in the morning.'

Your doctor might ask, 'Where does it hurt? When does it bother you? When did you first notice it? How much does it hurt?' But good doctors don't stop there. They also ask questions about what the problem is *not*. For example, your doctor would probably ask, 'Does it hurt anywhere else?' and 'Have you ever had this pain before?'

From asking questions, your doctor might discover that your problem is in your right elbow, and not any other part of your body. It hurts all day; not only certain times of the day. The pain first started six weeks ago, and you never had it before – except when you were at school.

3. *Examine closely the* differences *between where the problem is and where it is not.*

If a problem exists in one area and not in another, the difference between the two areas can produce clues to help locate the cause. So you ask: 'What peculiar differences exist between where the problem is occurring, and where it is not occurring?' Or 'What is different about when the problem occurs and when it doesn't?'

In the doctor example from Step 2, by specifying what, where, when and to what extent the problem is and is not, your doctor is able to determine the particular differences. For example, the doctor might discover that you are right handed, and that you played tennis at school. Then, by determining the peculiar differences between what the problem is and is not, your doctor is able to look for changes in and around the differences.

4. *Look carefully for* changes *that have occurred in and around the environment of the problem.*
   Changes can cause problems. In fact, problems – by definition – are always caused by changes. Remember that problems where no change has occurred are not true problems. They are decisions that must be made or plans that should be implemented. For example, guess what your doctor discovered you were doing with your son every night after dinner for the past six weeks? Right! You have Young Wimbledon elbow.

5. *Develop 'probable cause statements' concerning the changes discovered in Step 4 by linking each change to the problem.*
   Every change will produce its own unique probable cause statement.

   In the doctor example, a probable cause statement would be:

   > 'Playing tennis with your child each night after dinner has resulted in tendinitis in your elbow.'

6. *Test each probable cause statement against all of the* is *and* is not *facts, in order to determine the most probable cause.*
   For example, your doctor could say:

   > 'If it is tendinitis, would that account for the fact that the pain is in the right elbow and not the left?' Yes. 'That it hurts constantly and not only at certain times in the day?' Yes. 'That the pain first started six weeks ago and you have never had it before except when you were a tennis player at school?' Yes.

   Since tendinitis checks out against the known set of facts, the doctor would then move to the next step – veryifying that it really is the cause.

7. *Verify the most probable cause to make sure it is the real cause.*
   Your doctor could verify the cause by gently probing your elbow, or even taking X-rays.

Note that these seven steps are usually inexpensive: they just require mental effort – pencil and paper, and possibly phone calls to gather information. Of course, taking action to remedy the problem may involve financial commitment. And many lost pounds if you fail to go carefully through the problem-solving process!

Yet many people start their problem-solving efforts by throwing money into an ill-conceived solution before thinking through the problem. They jump in with both feet to take action. Any action! And they often end up spending far more time and money than is necessary – and the problem still isn't solved.

In brief outline, the seven-step process looks like this:

1. Problem statement: ______________________

2.	**IS**	**IS NOT**	**3. Difference**	**4. Changes**
What?	_____	_____	_______	_______
—Defect	_____	_____	_______	_______
—Object	_____	_____	_______	_______
Where?	_____	_____	_______	_______
When?	_____	_____	_______	_______
Extent?	_____	_____	_______	_______

2. Probable causes: 1. ______________________
2. ______________________
3. ______________________

6. Test the probable cause statements against the initial set of facts.

7. Verify the most probable cause.

Now let's illustrate the seven-step problem-solving technique by taking a hypothetical example. My American friend, Joe, tells the story:

The case of the sodden sheets

It has been a long hot day at the office, and I breathe a sigh of relief as I finish writing up the last paragraph of an eight-page report my boss asked for yesterday. Because of the unusually warm spell at the end of winter, the office has been hot and sticky all day. No time for relaxing tonight, either, because the PTA meeting starts at 8.30pm. Before that, I have to drive over to the Men's Store and pick up my new suit so I will have it for a special meeting tomorrow. And sometime during the running around I want to eat supper with the family. Fortunately, at least, no evening trip to the doctor tonight – the kids have been a lot better since I installed a new humidifier on the basement heating system two months ago.

The phone rings, I answer, it's my wife. She is really upset! She tells me there's a leak in the bedroom ceiling which is making a wet patch in the plaster that's getting bigger and bigger. She put a bucket on the floor under the leak and wants to know how soon I can get home. I tell her I'm on my way.

As I leave the car park, I am thinking about the leak – and how tight I am for time. A number of solutions come into my mind. I could shovel the snow off the roof, or call a plumber or a roofer. Or just empty the bucket every day. Or do nothing and let the bed get wet! One thing is certain, at least: the vice chairman is going to run the school PTA meeting tonight!

The bedroom ceiling's surface is textured plaster, I think to myself. If the drip continues, there will be a hole in the ceiling. And I can't fix a hole in textured plaster (rough finish with a swirled pattern). I'll have to replace the entire ceiling.

What should I do about the leak?

Well, I think, I can't jump to conclusions or do anything until the *cause* of the problem is determined. 'Calling a plumber' implies I know there is a leak in the water system. 'Shovelling snow off the roof' or 'calling a roofer' suggests that there's a hole in the roof. But since the cause of the problem is not known, the first thing to do is determine the most probable cause.

The attic floor was not made for walking on (we couldn't store boxes up there) so I have never been up there. Access to the attic is through a hatch in the ceiling of the landing; and using a step ladder, I crawl up into the attic, torch in hand. Directing the light to the roof area above the bedroom, what do I see? Nothing! That's right, nothing. The attic floor is perfectly dry.

'That's strange,' I say to myself. 'There's water down in the bedroom – and it's dry up here!' I then direct the light to the outside attic wall and see a remarkable sight. Ice! Thick ice covering the wall. 'Look at that ice!' I think to myself. 'And if there's ice on that wall, there must be ice at the other end of the attic too.' I let the torch shine towards the other end – and guess what? *No* ice. I think, 'Now this is really strange. There's ice on one wall, but no ice on the other.'

I think to myself, 'If there's ice on the west wall, and no ice on the east, there's obviously a reason for it. There must be some difference between the west end of the attic and the east end.' Then I notice that the west end of the attic seems less dark than the east end. Looking more closely, I suddenly become aware that there is no insulation over the place where the bedroom light fixture is – and I can see light shining through from the bedroom.

'All right,' I think, 'The heat from the bedroom could account for moist air condensing and freezing on the west wall, while not on the east. But why this year and not previous years? What has changed, causing this difference in the two walls?'

This problem can be made 'visible' be describing it in writing:

	The problem is	**The problem is not**	**Difference**	**Change**
What	Water	Dryness		
Where	Bedroom	Any other room		
	Bedroom ceiling	Attic floor		
	Ice on west wall	Ice on east wall	In insulation	None
When	This year	Previous year		
Extent	Very serious (to replace entire ceiling: over £1000)	OK		

What do you think has changed? Which single element has changed to cause this 'Case of the sodden sheets'? Yes – the new humidifier! And this is what the problem specification now looks like:

	The problem is	The problem is not	Difference	Change
What	Water	Dryness		
Where	Bedroom	Any other room		
	Bedroom ceiling	Attic floor		
	Ice on west wall	Ice on east wall	In insulation	None
When	This year	Previous years	MOISTURE	NEW HUMIDI-FIER
Extent	Very serious (to replace entire ceiling: over £1000)	OK		

The analysis is now ready for Step 5: write out a 'probable cause statement'. After the above analysis, here is what a probable cause statement will look like:

CHANGE ⟶ COMMONSENSE LINK ⟶ END RESULT

New humidifier installed last year increased moisture content in the air.	The warm, moist air rose through the uninsulated light fixture in the master bedroom.	The air froze with the winter weather and is now thawing during the current warm spell.

In Step 6, the probable cause statement will be tested against all the 'is' and 'is not' facts to determine if it fits the problem's specification. Say, 'If the new humidifier is causing the problem, does that explain . . .'

Water rather than dryness? Yes!
In the bedroom and not in any other room? Yes!
On the bedroom ceiling and not the attic floor? Yes!
Ice on the attic's west wall and not on the east one? Yes!
This year and not previous years? Yes!

Since the answer is 'Yes' to each set of 'is' and 'is not' facts, it appears that this probable cause tests positive against the known problem description.

But it is not certain that the new humidifier is the only cause – not yet! For there is one more – very important – step in the problem analysis process: verification! This can be achieved by asking additional questions, and obtaining additional information to see if it is the *real* cause.

Verification in this example might be as simple as calling a couple of local humidifier distributors and asking them if they have ever encountered this problem before. Or by looking up several humidifier installers in the phone book, and asking them if they have ever encountered an ice problem relating to a humidifier.

When it is reasonably certain that the most probable cause is *the* cause, then – and only then – is the time to take action. In this case, the short-term action was to remove the remaining ice from the attic wall. The long-term solution was to place insulation above the light fixture.

As you can see from our example, there is a direct relationship between the cause of a problem and the observed effects. The effects point to a very particular kind of problem, and that special problem would produce only those effects.

As you've seen, the cause of any problem leaves an imprint of effects that can be viewed in four dimensions. The first dimension is *identity*. In the 'Case of the sodden sheets', the problem's identity was a wet spot in the ceiling. The second dimension is *location*. The problem occurred in the bedroom ceiling, not in the attic floor – or in any other room. There is also a dimension of *timing*. The problem occurred this year, not in previous years.

And last, there is the *extent* of the problem – that is, its size and severity. In the case above, with a rough textured ceiling the old plaster could not simply be patched. The entire ceiling would need to be replaced, which would lead to major expenditure! So this problem was serious. But because it was analysed carefully, and verified by using the above problem-solving process, the action taken cost only the price of a little insulation (pennies) – rather that £1000 plus, and no effective solution to the problem!

One more point. Problems that fit the criteria of a problem (deviation from the standard, unknown cause, you are concerned about it) don't stay problems for long. You normally find the causes and fix them. But when you identify a list of existing problems, you will often find that your list includes a number of old problems. These old problems usually have known causes, but haven't been solved simply because you are unable to make decisions about them. These problems are not true problems at all. They require decisions (which will be covered in the next chapter), not problem-solving.

In this chapter you have seen the:

- importance of thinking through a problem before attempting to solve it;
- need to make the problem visible in writing;
- great value of using a problem-solving process;
- importance of not jumping to conclusions and taking premature, costly action.

A problem-solving process allows you to isolate the problem by describing what, where, when and to what extent the problem *is* and *is not*. You then know that the problem lies within this boundary. You need only ask the right questions – What? Where? When? and to what Extent?

Here's an outline of the process:

1. Problem statement
'What is wrong?'

2. Description

What defect?	'What symptoms do we have?'
	'What symptoms don't we have that we might expect?'
What object?	'What/who has failed?'
	'What/who has not failed?'
Where?	'Where do we have the problem?'
	'Where don't we have the problem?'
When?	'When did it start?'
	'When was everything OK?'
Extent?	'How serious is it?'
	'How big is it?'
	'What is normal?'

3. Differences?

'What is strange/different/unusual/peculiar about this problem?'

	'Why is it doing this, and not that?' 'Why did this fail, and not that?' 'Why did it happen here, and not there?' 'Why did it start then and not before?' 'Why is it this much bigger or more serious than normal?'
4. Changes?	'What has changed?' 'How has it changed?' 'When did it change?'
5. Probable causes?	'How could this change cause the problem?'
6. Mentally testing	'If this is the cause, does it explain all the facts of our problem description?'
7. Verification	'Who else can we talk to, what records can we check, what evidence can we find to determine that this is the real cause of our problem?'

Try using the seven-step problem-solving grid on the following page to solve some problems you have. You may find blanks in the grid. Since many people are task-orientated and want to solve the problem immediately, these can cause frustration. This is not only a normal reaction; it is often a positive one, since it gives you a clear direction about where to go and whom to ask for the missing information. In other words, the grid process protects you from jumping to conclusions and taking the right action on the wrong cause!

By using this seven-step diagnostic process, you can resolve problems more quickly; correct causes, not just effects; solve problems so that they stay solved; and not create new problems by taking the wrong action.

A problem exists when: (1) a deviation from an expected standard has occurred; (2) the cause of the deviation is uncertain; and (3) the deviation concerns you.

1. PROBLEM STATEMENT ______________________________

		2. IS	IS NOT	3. DIFFERENCES	4. CHANGES
WHAT?	DEFECT (Symptoms)				
WHAT?	OBJECT (Who/What?)				
	WHERE?				
	WHEN?				
	EXTENT? (Seriousness)				

STEPS IN DIAGNOSING CAUSE

1. Write a specific negative problem statement.
2. Describe the problem by writing what, where, when and to what extent the problem IS and IS NOT.
3. Determine any peculiar and pertinent differences between what the problem IS and what the problem IS NOT.
4. Look carefully for changes that have occurred in and around the differences.
5. Write a probable cause statement for each change discovered in step 4 above.
6. Test each probable cause statement against each specific set of IS and IS NOT facts, and determine the most probable cause.
7. Verify the most probable cause statement, take appropriate action, and monitor results.

5. PROBABLE CAUSE STATEMENTS (one for each change)			6. Test each probable cause statement against each set of 'IS' and 'IS NOT' facts.
CHANGE	LINK	END RESULT	

7. Most probable cause statements: ______________________________

— What can be done to verify that this is the cause? ______________________________

— Given that this is the cause, what action(s) can be taken to correct the original problem? ______________________________

Chapter 7

Making Good Decisions

Charles Kepner and Benjamin Tregoe have greatly influenced the field of modern decision-making. They have formulated their ideas into a four-stage process – called the 'Kepner-Tregoe (KT) Decision Analysis.' These four steps are:

1. Write a decision statement.
2. Develop objectives.
3. Create alternatives.
4. Examine risks.

Let's look at the Kepner-Tregoe process, beginning with some important ideas how to write a decision statement.

1. Writing a decision statement

As with problem solving, the first step is to make the decision statement visible – write it down. So let's begin by examining how to write this statement.

One mistake that is easy to make when writing decision statements is to write statements which require the reader to take an immediate stand. These statements are decisions like: 'Accept or reject that proposal'; 'Go to Bristol or not'; 'Vote "yes" or "no" on fire-arms control'; or, 'Give up the job or not'. These statements, by the way they are worded, tend to force your thinking into a premature comparison of only two alternatives.

To make more effective decisions, keep your statements open for more than two choices. For example, you could take the decision statement, 'Accept or reject that proposal', and rewrite it to give you other alternatives. If you start decision statements with the words, 'Select the best . . .' you are almost guaranteed to have an 'open' decision statement. Thus, the first statement above can be written, 'Select the best proposal'. And the second decision statement, 'Go to Bristol or not', becomes 'Select the best city to visit'. Now you are free to choose: to go to London, Bristol, York – or stay at home.

How could you turn 'Vote "yes" or "no" on fire-arms control' into an open decision statement? Sometimes it helps to ask yourself a question like, 'Why would someone want fire-arms control?' (We're not taking a stand here.) Now note that fire-arms control is one possible solution to at least two different problems – reducing crime and preventing gun accidents. But as Dr Peter Drucker said, 'Trying to solve two problems with one solution very seldom works.'

Rather than limiting your decision statement to only one solution, it is better to find the main problems being faced, and to put each problem's solution in its own decision statement. This allows you to develop a list of alternative solutions for each decision statement.

Problems	*High crime rate*	*Fire-arms accidents*
Decision Statements	Select best way to reduce crime.	Select best way to reduce fire-arms accidents.
Alternatives	1. Fire-arms control 2. Stiffer penalties 3. More police 4. Better security	1. Fire-arms control 2. Education 3. 'Safety' ammunition 4. Child-proof guns

Notice the many choices made available by making decision statements 'open'. You could still implement fire-arms control if you wish. But by transforming your initial fire-arms control statement into two pertinent open statements, you open up a variety of courses of action.

2. Developing objectives

Step 2 in decision-making is to decide what you want to accomplish by your decision – your goals, objectives, desired results – before creating alternative solutions. Developing objectives before alternatives counteracts the tendency to choose only those objectives which fit your pre-selected solutions.

Get help from others in writing out your list of objectives. And include all important items that are considerations in making the decision. The more sound information you have here, the better your final decision will be.

Objectives come from questions like these:

'What factors should I consider?'
Examples:
- Time
- Approvals
- Location

'What results are desired?'
Examples:
- Efficiency
- Safety
- Recognition
- Saving money
- Satisfaction
- High morale

'What resources are available?'
Examples:
- People
- Equipment
- Skills
- Budget
- Materials
- Knowledge

'What restrictions are there?
Examples:
- Law
- Standards
- Ethics
- Policy
- Values

Before going on the the last two steps, let's look at an example of decision-making. Read the following case study, noting what you feel are the important objectives in this situation.

The case of the difficult dwelling decision

Matt and his wife Kathleen sat at the kitchen table talking about their decision to buy a home. Their lease would expire in four months, the house had been sold and the new owners were eager to move in.

Matt knew that Kathleen was looking forward to leaving their cramped three-bedroomed house. With four children – two girls, aged 5 and 16, and two boys 9 and 15 – it had really been hard for her. It had also been hard on the teenage children, who had to share their rooms with their younger siblings. But the boys were a particular problem for Kathleen. They fought constantly, each blaming the other for making the room untidy, and neither accepting responsibility for clearing it up. Fortunately, they had a large garden for the dogs!

Matt hoped that they could locate a house they could afford with at least half an acre of garden. If they could get a 90 per cent mortgage, they could manage it. It would use up all their savings; and with no way of borrowing extra money for emergencies, it would be risky. But it would be well worth it.

Matt also hoped they could get a garage that would house the boat, because he hated leaving it out in the rain. And Kathleen wanted at least two bathrooms. In fact, she said that if a house didn't have two full bathrooms, she wouldn't even consider it. She was sick of 'Waterloo Station,' as she called their single bathroom. And wherever the house was, it must have public sewage, water, and gas. Matt had sworn never to have a septic tank again. And all their appliances were gas.

It would also be nice to be located within a couple of miles of a shopping centre. One redeeming factor about their present home was its location only a few minutes walk from a small shopping centre.

Fortunately, since the schools in the area were excellent, they were not a problem.

To get the size of home they wanted for the money they had to spend, Matt knew they would have to buy a property which was a considerable distance from town. He didn't mind the drive – so long as the house wasn't more than 45 minutes from work on the motorway and he didn't have to drive with the sun in his eyes in the morning and evening.

Thus, Matt and Kathleen's objectives in buying a home are the following:

1. Available in four months
2. Minimum of four bedrooms
3. Large garden
4. 90 per cent mortgage available
5. Garage for the boat
6. Two bathrooms
7. Public utilities (sewage, water, gas)
8. Near a shopping centre
9. Not more than 45 minutes from work
10. Not west of the city.

When a list of objectives has been established, the next step is to determine which of them are *required* and which are simply *desired*. Then when you later develop alternative solutions, each solution must meet the required objectives or it is not acceptable. This will save lots of time and energy by limiting your thought and discussion only to those alternatives that actually meet your required objectives.

'Must' objectives are established by basic needs, budget, time, policy, rules and law. 'Want' objectives are often comparisons, such as low cost, least time, largest, nicest, best, etc.

Because 'must' objectives limit alternatives, it is wise to restrict their number when possible. Musts also need to be specific and measurable (eg., 'Available in four months', not 'Available soon').

Looking at the list above, which items do you think were Matt and Kathleen's *must* objectives and which were their *want* objectives?

If you were making this judgement for yourself, of course, your *must* and *want* objectives would probably be different from Matt and Kathleen's. In their case, however, they felt that 'Available in four months,' 'Minimum of four bedrooms,' '90 per cent mortgage available,' and 'Two bathrooms' were their *musts*.

3. Creating alternatives

In this step you create alternatives to fulfil your objectives. At this point, it is often helpful to think in terms of the following classifications:

- *corrective* alternatives that solve the problem;
- *interim* alternatives that don't remedy the problem, but do buy time; and
- *adaptable* alternatives which allow us to live with the problem.

For example, if the problem is a fire, I can take corrective action by putting the fire out with water. Or I could take interim action by doing something to restrict air flow to the fire. Or I could take adaptive action by deciding to let the building burn down. By being aware of all three of these classes of alternatives, we can significantly increase the number of available approaches.

In developing creative alternatives, two things are helpful. First, 'brainstorm' a list of possibilities, and later evaluate and combine them to create workable solutions. Second, get help! Talk to people whose opinions and judgements you trust. Since you have made your decision process visible (in writing) from the beginning, you can show others both the problem and the alternatives you are considering, and ask them for additional ideas.

It is much easier to make good decisions after you have clarified your objectives and created alternatives. For example, consider the 'Case of the difficult dwelling decision' just presented. Evaluate the following three alternatives, given Matt and Kathleen's list of objectives. Should any of these homes be eliminated because it fails to satisfy at least one of their *must* objectives?

1. An attractive new three-storey house, with a big garden, four bedrooms (and a possible fifth bedroom in the attic), and two bathrooms. 90 per cent mortgage. No garage. Gas and sewage available. Approximately 15 miles from work. No shopping centre nearby. Possession immediate. Located in an established, older neighbourhood.
2. A new house that Matt really likes, with four bedrooms and a large two-car garage. In addition, it has two bathrooms, a shopping centre five minutes' walk away, 90 per cent mortgage available, a small garden, and gas and sewage. It is only 30 minutes from work, and will be available in three months. Unfortunately, its location will mean that Matt will have to drive to and from work with the sun in his eyes.
3. The third house is Kathleen's choice, even though it is not new. It is about six years old, with five bedrooms and two bathrooms, and is in a beautiful neighbourhood. The extremely large garden has many trees (with a swing for the children), and a tree house), and a good high fence for the dogs. Matt also likes the fully established garden, with a single garage and tool shed at the back; and the fact that it is only six miles from work. A 90 per cent mortgage can be obtained. A shopping centre and the primary school are only a few minutes walk away. Gas and public sewage are available. The present owners have kept the house spotless. But they are building a new home and hope to move out within four months. For the asking price, the house is a bargain.

Must any of these three homes be eliminated from consideration because it fails to meet Matt and Katheen's *must* objectives?

Matt and Kathleen are faced with a difficult decision. Emotionally, they want house 3. But they really cannot consider this alternative, because it doesn't meet one of their *must* objectives – 'Available in four months'. Earlier we said that it is not desirable to have *must* objectives that are not absolutely necessary, because they eliminate alternatives. So unless Matt and Kathleen can find a way out of their dilemma by making the four months a *want* objective, they cannot select this alternative – and must confine their attention to houses 1 and 2, both of which meet all their *must* objectives.

This decision is typical of the ones you face at work as well as at home. Emotionally, you want to select a particular alternative –

and too often do, even when the absence of *must* qualities suggests it will not work out well. Decisions turn out better when you first take the time to determine objectives, prioritise them, create a number of alternatives, and then rationally evaluate each one in terms of *musts*. This process produces good decisions because it helps you to work out what is really important.

4. Analysing risk

The fourth and last step in the decision process is to consider carefully the risk involved with each of the leading alternatives. This is the most neglected step in decision-making – because we tend to look at life's new possibilities and beginnings in glowing terms. You must examine the risks in your decisions before implementing them. To do this, simply ask, 'What can go wrong?' And here again, seek out help from others with experience, since several individuals can often foresee future problems better than one person working alone.

When first considering potential risks, deal with one alternative at a time. That is, do not attempt initially to look at the possibility of each risk occurring in every alternative. Then when you have completed your list of potential risks (problems) for the first alternative, evaluate each potential problem in terms of the probability of it happening, and its seriousness if it does happen. Then repeat the same process with each of your other leading alternatives.

In the 'Case of the difficult dwelling decision', Matt and Kathleen were left with two alternatives – homes 1 and 2. Their last step, then, was to evaluate the risks in selecting each of these alternatives by asking: 'If we buy this particular house, what could go wrong?' After talking to friends and some professionals, they developed the following 'risk list'. (Note that even though we show the following risks together in one chart, each alternative's risks should be analysed separately.)

Alternative 1: Risks	*Probability* (of its happening)	*Seriousness* (if it happens)
1. Builder has a poor reputation; this house may turn out to be a white elephant.	LOW	HIGH
2. Three-storey houses are difficult to heat.	HIGH	LOW

	Probability (of its happening)	*Seriousness* (if it happens)
3. Since this is a new house in an established neighbourhood, we might get complaints about our dogs. (We didn't see any other dogs when we drove around.)	MEDIUM	MEDIUM
4. When we looked at the house on Saturday, we didn't notice many children either. How will the neighbours feel about four active children?	LOW	MEDIUM
Alternative 2: Risks		
1. Expensive fire insurance since the house is weatherboarded.	HIGH	LOW

Though we can't make Matt and Kathleen's decision for them, their own evaluation of risks suggests that alternative 2 may be the best house for their needs because of the greater number of potential problems with alternative 1.

This four-step process – writing an 'open' decision statement, developing objectives, creating and evaluating alternatives, and analysing risk – is usually the best way to make a well-balanced decision.

But there are, of course, always exceptions. Therefore, we will conclude this chapter by looking briefly at another decision-making technique, especially useful when the decision involves only two alternatives or deals with less logical factors than normal.

Force field analysis

'Force field analysis' is, in fact, a simple and easy way to make good decisions. You need only to think of – and make visible – all the reasons for choosing one alternative, and then all the reasons for not doing so.

Let's look at a typical example. Suppose you are deciding whether or not to seek promotion to supervisor. Your decision can be drawn like this:

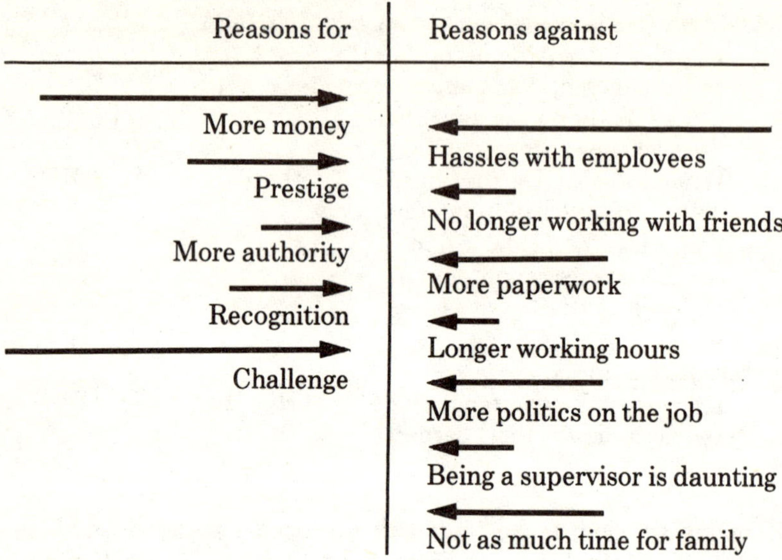

The length of the arrow indicates the relative importance of this factor to you. Analyse each factor for:

1. *Realism* (Is it a fact? Your opinion? A rumour?)
2. *Control* (Can you do anything about this factor? Make a positive element even more positive? Or a negative factor less negative?

As in the four-step decision-making process, seek help! Talk to people who have faced similar decisions in the past. Ask them about additional factors to consider, and use their insight to evaluate the relative strength of each of your factors.

The following two pages are work sheets for first, the four-step decision-making process, and then the force field analysis. Try using them to make a decision you currently face.

The four-step decision process
Work sheet

Decision statement ____
____
____

Objectives:		Must have	Want to have
	______________	______	______
	______________	______	______
	______________	______	______
	______________	______	______
	______________	______	______
	______________	______	______
	______________	______	______
	______________	______	______
	______________	______	______

Alternatives: 1. ____
____

2. ____
____

3. ____
____

4. ____
____

Risks with leading alternatives

(Rate each risk in terms of the Probability of its happening, and its Seriousness if it does happen, using H = High, M = Medium, and L = Low.)

Alternative	P	S	Alternative	P	S
	(H, M, L)			(H, M, L)	
__________	____	____	__________	____	____
__________	____	____	__________	____	____
__________	____	____	__________	____	____
__________	____	____	__________	____	____
__________	____	____	__________	____	____

Force field analysis
Work sheet

Draw horizontal arrows on each side of the vertical line corresponding to the reasons for (left side), and the reasons against (right side) your decision.

Use the arrow's length to indicate the relative importance of each reason.

Seek help; talk to others.

Decision statement: ______________________________
____
____

Reasons for	Reasons against

Analyse each factor for realism. Is it a fact? Your opinion? A rumour? How could you verify those factors that are opinions or rumours?

____
____
____

What factors can you control, ie., how can you make a positive factor even more positive? Or a negative factor less negative?

____
____
____

Chapter 8

The Importance of Planning

Good planning is based on a four-stage process:

- determining your goals and setting priorities
- writing your priority goals in an objective form
- developing steps to reach your objectives
- anticipating potential problems.

In this chapter, we will review each of these stages of successful planning. Then you can use the work sheet at the end of the chapter to practise planning your work – or any of your ambitions.

In all human activity, planning is critical for several important reasons.

1. *Knowing where you are going helps you get there.* Alice said to the Cheshire cat in Lewis Carroll's *Through the Looking Glass*:

    'Tell me, please, which way it is I ought to go from here.'
    'Where is it you want to go?' said the cat.
    'I don't care much where,' said Alice.
    'Then it doesn't matter which way you go!' said the cat.

The cat was telling Alice that it didn't make much difference what she did, since she didn't know where she wanted to go. But it makes a very great difference at work to know where you want to go. If you are not moving towards a specific goal, you have no way of knowing whether your work is productive or not. Successful people plan everything they do – every day. Plans make destinations clear. They suggest how to get there, and they allow you to measure the success of your efforts.

2. *Planning enables you to experience a daily sense of accomplishment.* Your plans will guide you in choosing the work today that will lead to your goals – thus providing a continuous feeling of fulfilment. Distant, general aims alone don't have much

personal influence on your immediate activities. But when you take a distant goal and specify the steps you have to take to reach that goal as well as a detailed plan to reach each step, then you'll see that certain of these steps need to be worked on this week – or today. By successfully carrying out today's steps in your plan, you are immediately rewarded with a sense of accomplishment.

3. *Good planning prevents procrastination.* The most important things in life (like distant goals and objectives) do not create a sense of urgency until you begin to see how to reach them. Because they appear so far in the future, you may feel it is all right to put off action on them until tomorrow – especially since there are so many seemingly urgent things to do right now. So, given the choice between 'urgent' matters and distant aims (no matter how important), most people normally go with the urgent and postpone the important. But when you bring your ultimate goals and objectives into the present by creating step-by-step plans, then you may realise that acting towards the achievement of a goal is urgent now.
4. *Planning prevents problems.* Well thought-out plans help you to anticipate potential problems before they happen. Problems are much less likely to happen if you take the time to analyse them by thinking them through, talking to others, and developing creative solutions.

Most people agree that good planning is essential to the success of any project. And yet, all too often, we don't spend sufficient time in planning. Why not? There are a number of reasons:

- You may have to commit yourself to doing something today that you really don't want to do. And so, 'No problem is so big that it can't be ignored'!
- You can seem like a 'hero' by putting out fires caused through lack of planning. You can even make a career out of permitting crises which you then step into and dramatically end.
- It simply seems easier to operate by working on your feet and bouncing along from one crisis to the next.
- It takes time to write goal statements and then develop plans and strategies.
- Your performance at work is often evaluated in terms of what you appear to be *doing*, rather than how well you plan. For

example, you are sitting at your desk planning how best to do a high priority task, and your boss walks up and says, 'Don't just sit there. Get busy and *do* something!'
- You may not know how to plan effectively.

So let's look at the steps in good planning.

Determining your goals and setting priorities

The first step in real planning is to find a quiet place and think up a list of the most important things you want to do and be. As you list your goals, don't stop to evaluate or judge them. Write down everything that occurs to you, even it it may seem silly. If you have a burning secret desire - write it down! Look at all areas of your life, not just your job. Consider family, education, work, hobbies, personal growth - whatever goals are important to you.

Don't worry about writing measurable objective statements at this point. As long as you know what you mean by what you have written, that's fine. And this is *your* list; don't show it to anybody.

For example, here is my list of personal goals:

1. Improve my relationship with my children*
2. Write another book
3. Gross £X next year
4. Attend the next International Training Federation meeting
5. Take a canoe trip on a fast-flowing river
6. Audition for a part in our local theatre's annual production
7. Visit three foreign countries next year
8. Buy a 1960s Beetle
9. Learn how to fly
10. Try gliding
11. Be a good grandfather
12. Visit my son in Australia
13. Limit my work trips away from home to no more than four a year
14. Build a cider press before next autumn
15. Build a small boat to use for messing about on the river
16. Learn Russian*
17. Perform a solo guitar piece in the approaching Christmas music festival
18. Put more time and effort into my marriage*
19. Lose a stone in weight

After you have spent a few minutes creating your personal goal list, select the top three items and mark them with an asterisk or a tick (as I have). You can use the form below to create your list of what you most want to do and be.

My personal and job-related goals

Don't stop to judge or evaluate your goals as you write them down. Just list those things you want to do, be or become, as they occur to you. Consider all areas of your life: business; family; education; hobbies; religion; etc for other possibilities.

1. ______________________________
2. ______________________________
3. ______________________________
4. ______________________________
5. ______________________________
6. ______________________________
7. ______________________________
8. ______________________________
9. ______________________________
10. ______________________________
11. ______________________________
12. ______________________________
13. ______________________________
14. ______________________________
15. ______________________________
16. ______________________________
17. ______________________________
18. ______________________________

Now put a tick or asterisk beside your top three goals at this time in your life.

Writing your priority goals in an objective form

Now that you have thought of a list of the things you would like to be and do, and identified the most important ones, you are ready to enter into an eight-step planning process. The first step is to write out your highest-priority goals in an objective form.

An objective (or goal – we will use these two words interchangeably) is simply a statement of exactly what you want to accomplish. Such a statement should have the following three characteristics:

1. An objective statement should be *specific*, not general. For example, the statement: 'Improve my relationship with my children' does not communicate enough information. How am I going to try to improve my relationship with them? What areas am I going to work on? How will I know when I have improved my relationship with them? By what date do I want to see such improvement? And what does the word 'relationship' mean? Since my objective statement doesn't give enough specific information about my goal, it will be hard to actually know when I am successful – or even whether I am unsuccessful. So in my objective statement I need to:

   - Determine what *actions* I am going to take – what I will do – to improve my relationship with my children. I need to specify certain behaviour. For example, I could:
     — Read one *recommended book on bringing up children and one on the problems of adolescence by 1 December;*
     — *Attend at least one school activity involving each child this term;*
     — *Quietly, attentively, ask each of the children how everything is going – every day, when possible.*
   - *Identify end results*. For example:
     — By next school year, each of the children will be taking the initiative to invite me to particular school activities;
     — Each child will be voluntarily coming to confide in me concerning his or her problems, hopes, etc.

2. A good objective statement should be *measurable* or *quantifiable*. To 'learn Russian', sounds fine. But I really won't know when I have satisfactorily achieved this goal, because I haven't indicated my standard – or measure – of achievement. If I rewrite it, stating, 'Obtain a diploma in Russian from London University

within two years,' my goal is measurable in two ways. First, I have use a word that specifies *behaviour* (speaking, rather than learn). And second, I have committed myself to a specific *period*. With my goal statement re-expressed in measurable terms, I will be able to determine when I have achieved it.

3. Third, an objective statement should be truly *achievable*. There is little point in setting yourself up for failure. A good goal statement will extend and improve you, not break you. For example, note that my objective is to learn how to speak, not write Russian. As a dyslexic, my spelling skills in English are limited. For me to learn how to spell Russian words correctly would be nearly impossible! If I wrote a goal statement on writing Russian, I'd be setting myself up for failure.

You can develop several different types of job objectives:

- First are regular or *routine* objectives that simply specify the things you normally do at work.
- Second are *problem-solving* objectives that you write to solve a specific problem.
- Next are *innovative* objectives, written to facilitate new or creative ideas.
- Finally come *personal* objectives, which you write about yourself.

Since most of your development at work is connected with the last three kinds of objective, it will be beneficial both to you and your organisation to concentrate more of your efforts in these three areas, rather than on routine objectives.

Before you start to spend time working on your job-related objectives, it would be best to sit down with your boss and enquire what he or she feels about your priorities. Ask which of the objectives you have written are 'must do', 'ought to do', and 'nice to do'. Since your performance will be appraised in the future on what you do, it only makes sense to complete job objectives that meet with your boss's approval.

Put your energies into only two or three objectives at any one time. Your chances of success are much better if you concentrate on a few important ones rather than all at once. (Other less important objectives can usually be addressed in the future.)

Make copies of the 'Planning work sheet' at the end of this chapter. Use one work sheet for each of your key objectives. Write your objectives in specific and measurable terms so that you and others are aware of when you have reached them.

Developing steps to reach your objectives

After you have determined which objectives you want to implement, you can then develop the steps you will take to achieve these objectives. As you identify the steps in your plan, set completion dates for each step. (But do not assign a final number to your steps at this point. You may need to add more steps later.)

As an example, I know a person – let's call her 'Elizabeth' – whose objective was to become a supervisor in her organisation within two years. The initial steps of her plan looked something like this:

1. **Objective**
   To become a supervisor in my organisation within two years.
2. **Steps of plan** (with completion dates)

Step	Date
Have a meeting with my boss to discuss my goal.	15 Jun
Write three key objectives in my present job, and discuss these with my boss.	30 Jun
Attend evening classes and acquire the credits I need to finish my part-time degree, starting this academic year.	15 Sept
Analyse my leadership skills; determine my strengths and where I need improvement.	15 Oct
Sign up for at least one supervisory workshop (each year) at the local training management centre.	1 Dec
Determine which supervisory positions might be available within two years.	1 Mar

Anticipating potential problems in your plans

Now you need to look carefully at the steps in your plan, noting any that could cause difficulties – let's call them 'critical' steps. From past experience, sometimes you *know* that a particular step means trouble! (Maybe you took that step before and it led to a disaster.) If a step is completely new to you, look out. 'Murphy's Law' may get you! Major steps, involving lots of bits and pieces, are especially subject to the rule that 'What can go wrong, will go wrong', particularly if you have no experience of the step. You have also probably noted that problems can result when people have to communicate over distances by telephone or letter; and also when there are a number of people involved.

If a step means operating close to the limits of your space, time or money, you probably have trouble brewing. For example, if your plan requires that you order a new item that is exactly 3 feet wide, and your door is 3 feet and half an inch, you had better get an axe out! Or if someone tells you the item you ordered will be here on Wednesday and you have to have it on Thursday, you might be wise to assume that it won't arrive until Friday. If a step in your plan 'will only cost £99.95', and you have exactly £100.00, then you pretty well know what's going to happen!

All this potential problem analysis may sound negative. But the good news is that if you can anticipate potential problems before you implement your plan, you can often develop solutions that will increase the chances that you will achieve your goal.

In the example of Elizabeth, she selected as a critical step in her plan, 'Attend evening classes and obtain the credits I need to finish my degree.' She viewed this step as a problem because it was new for her (she had never attended evening classes before). It was also a very important one. She worked for a boss who had once said in her presence, 'Your chances of being selected as a supervisor in this organisation are a lot greater if you have had further education.'

Next, look at the steps that may cause problems (critical steps), and list the potential problems. In Elizabeth's case, she wrote down the following problems:

3. Critical step

'Attend evening classes and obtain the credits I need to finish my degree, starting this academic year.'

4. Potential problems

A. Evening classes will be very hard on my family.
B. I'll get bored and stop attending.
C. It may take longer than two years to get the credits I need.

The next step is to evaluate the probability and seriousness of each potential problem. That is, work out what the probability is that the problem will occur, and how seriously it will affect the success of your plan if it does occur. To rate probability and seriousness, use H for high, M for medium and L for low.

In the example of Elizabeth, she felt that evening classes would be a hardship for her family – not only in terms of cost, but also time. Attending classes would reduce her time at home, and the courses would also require a great deal of time for homework.

She felt that the chances of her getting bored with the classes and dropping out were very low. But of course, if this did happen, it would have a serious impact on her plan, because her boss would see her as a failure in an area he considered very important. She thought she could finish the degree within the two-year time limit; and if she didn't, she would be so close to finishing that her boss would still support her efforts. Her analysis now looked like this:

4. Potential problems	**5. Evaluate each potential problem as to their probability and seriousness** (High, Medium, Low) P	S
A. Evening classes will be very hard on my family.	H	H
B. I'll get bored and stop attending.	L	H
C. It may take longer than two years to get the credits I need.	L	M

Now you need to analyse your greatest potential problem by finding likely causes, planning preventive action and planning contingency action. In solving problems, you act on causes. And to prevent, or be prepared for, potential problems, you look for likely causes. After you have identified the likely causes, ask, 'What can be done to reduce the probability that this event (or likely cause) will happen?' In other words, what preventive action can you include in your plans?

But you must also consider: 'If the worst comes to the worst and the problem does occur, what can I do now to reduce the seriousness of the consequences?' In other words, what contingency action can you include in your plans now?

In the case of Elizabeth, the potential problem 'Evening classes will be very hard on my family' has a high probability of happening; and when it happens, it will be high in seriousness.

6. Highest priority potential problem
'Evening classes will be very hard on my family.'

Likely Causes	Preventive Action	Contingency Action
Two nights per week away from family	See of Open University has distance courses I can take at home.	Enrol Bill (husband) in one or more courses with me.
Shortage of money	See if organisation will pay for all or part. Enrol in local authority institute rather than private college.	Borrow from relatives.
Lack of study time	Buy course books now and start studying in advance. Take courses that are easier for me.	Get family to help me study.
Family not aware of hardships	Involve family in pre-planning. Ask Bill to talk to Joe who is attending evening classes.	(No action)

7. Repeat steps 4–6 with any other critical step(s)
Elizabeth would then select other critical steps, and repeat Steps 4–6 by:

- Listing any potential problems concerning each critical step.
- Evaluating each potential problem as to its probability of happening and seriousness if it happens.

- Analysing each major potential problem for likely causes, preventive action, and contingency action.

The last – and highly important – step in planning is to build your preventive and contingency actions into your original plan at the appropriate points, with completion dates for each action.

In our example, Elizabeth's plan will now look like this:

8. Incorporate important preventive and contigency actions into your plan at the appropriate points

A. Have a family meeting to discuss educational plans.	1 Jun
B. Have a meeting with boss to discuss promotional goal, and determine whether the organisation will assist with tuition.	15 Jun
C. Write three key development objectives in my present job and discuss with boss.	30 Aug
D. Discuss plans with education officer at local institute of further education and identify required courses. Consider courses that Bill would enjoy taking. Also determine at this meeting if there are courses I can take at home.	15 Sept
E. Analyse my leadership skills; determine my strengths and where I need improvement.	15 Oct
Etc.	

By using this planning process, Elizabeth has greatly increased the probability of reaching her goal. Also note that some of her completion dates have changed in order to include her new activities. At this point (after incorporating the preventive/contingency actions concerning other high-priority problem), Elizabeth is now able to review her plans to make certain she really can meet her initial objective of being promoted to supervisor within two years.

Many of us spend a great deal of time dealing with a variety of problems, but doing very little planning. We can become so busy running from crisis to crisis that we don't take the time to plan for success – in, or outside, our jobs.

But when you commit yourself to identifying your goals, and follow a proven step-by-step plan to achieve them, you will find you are not sidetracked by problems – and will significantly increase your level of achievement.

On the following pages is a work sheet which will lead you through the eight-step planning process for achieving your major work – and life – objectives.

Planning work sheet

After writing down your goals (thinking them up without making judgements), and identifying those with the highest priority, select your most important goal and write it in specific, measurable terms, with a deadline. This is your objective statement.

1. **Objective** ______________________________
____

2. List the steps you should take to achieve this objective, with completion dates.

Steps of plan	**Date**
1. ______________________	______
2. ______________________	______
3. ______________________	______
4. ______________________	______
5. ______________________	______
6. ______________________	______
7. ______________________	______
8. ______________________	______
9. ______________________	______
10. ______________________	______

3. Analyse which steps have the highest risk of encountering problems. These are critical steps. Mark critical steps with an asterisk or a tick, and then write one of them below. (The following analysis will be repeated later for the other critical steps.)

Critical step ____

____

4. Answer the question, 'What can go wrong with this step?' by identifying potential problems.

5. **Evaluate each potential problem** as to its *probability* of happening, and *seriousness* if it happens, using H = High, M = Medium, L = Low

Potential problems	Probability	Seriousness
______________	________	________
______________	________	________
______________	________	________
______________	________	________
______________	________	________
______________	________	________

6. Analyse the highest priority potential problem with likely causes, and prevention and contingency action.

Highest priority potential problem ____________________

Likely causes	**Preventive action**	**Contingency action**

7. **Repeat steps 4–6 with any other critical step(s)** using copies of this worksheet.

8. **Incorporate important preventive and contingency actions** (from Step 6) as added steps in your original plan (Step 2). Write all steps in logical order and then number each step. Last, write a completion date for each step.

Step number	Step	Completion date

Chapter 9

Managing Your Time

Remember when we were young, and those lazy summer days stretched on and on? Remember how the closer it got to the summer holidays, the longer they took to arrive? Remember when the time from one holiday to the next seemed endless?

And now, why do our days seem hurried, almost mysteriously shortened? What happened? What happened to *time*?

Certainly our perception of time is dependent on what we're doing. We all know how waiting for something we want to happen seems like forever, and how a disagreeable task seems to take so long.

But that's only part of the answer. Our perception of time is also affected by the number of events we're conscious of in a given period. For example, a drive from point A to point B on an unfamiliar road may seem to take forever. But if we travel that same distance on a familiar road, the trip will seem shorter. When we are engaged in habitual tasks, we often wonder at the end of the day where the time has gone. The danger here is that we may not be aware of the way we have managed (or haven't managed) much of this routine time.

Most of us want to become increasingly effective in what we do. But the desire to improve is not all that is necessary. We also need to become aware of how we have been managing our time, so that we are able to understand what positive changes can be made, and why.

Time management is actually a matter of asking yourself some personal questions. The first is: 'What are the things that are truly important to me?' Second, 'How much of my time am I giving to those things?' And third, 'What uses up my time while contributing very little to my goal – or to the quality of my life?'

Time management also means accepting responsibility. It's easy to say, 'I have trouble managing my time because:

Other people always interrupt me.
Reports are misfiled by others.

There is too much paper work.
My boss changes his or her priorities.
Others won't cooperate with me.
There are too many emergency project requests.
The computer is always down.
It always seem as though I have to wait for others.'

Agreed – many of these problems do occur. But they happen to everybody! And we know that some people, facing all these problems, are much more productive than others.

Good time managers will surely appreciate Reinhold Niebuhr's prayer, '. . . grant me the serenity to accept the things I cannot change, courage to change the things I can, and the wisdom to know the difference.' Effective people have learned to accept the things they can't change, and to take responsibility for the things they can change. And they recognise the difference.

If you are able to exert some control in your life, to make certain decisions, and to accept part of the responsibility for what you do or don't do – then you can do something about your life. And it's *your* choice!

Awareness of time

Given that you have a positive attitude, that you want to be increasingly effective, and that you are willing to accept responsibility for change, what's next? What can you do to manage your time more productively? First, find out where you are.

Peter Drucker has said, 'Memory is treacherous; don't trust it.' That is, what you think you did and what you've really done are often two different things. So you must have some way of obtaining accurate information about past actions to use in decisions for future planning. The best method is to use a *time log* to record accurately how you are spending your time.

Reproduce copies of the time log on the following page, and use it to record your daily time expenditures. Record *everything* you do. Write down when you are interrupted and when you interrupt yourself. Note telephone calls, incoming and outgoing; visitors; trips to the bathroom; a coffee break. Write it all down! To obtain enough information for a complete analysis of your time, you should plan to record a minimum of three full days, both at work and at home.

Time log

Name ______________________________ **Date** ____________

Time	*Activity*	*Time taken*
____	______________________________	________
____	______________________________	________
____	______________________________	________
____	______________________________	________
____	______________________________	________
____	______________________________	________
____	______________________________	________
____	______________________________	________
____	______________________________	________
____	______________________________	________
____	______________________________	________
____	______________________________	________
____	______________________________	________
____	______________________________	________

When you have finished collecting information on how you actually spend your time, add up your time in categories. This will be a major help in determining whether the way you spend your time is really how you want to spend it. Using the following chart, categorise and record each day's information from your time log sheets.

	Day 1	Day 2	Day 3	Day 4	Day 5	Day 6	Day 7	TOTAL	%
Home									
Yourself	____	____	____	____	____	____	____	______	____
Spouse	____	____	____	____	____	____	____	______	____
Children	____	____	____	____	____	____	____	______	____
Friends	____	____	____	____	____	____	____	______	____
Chores	____	____	____	____	____	____	____	______	____
Eating	____	____	____	____	____	____	____	______	____
Sleeping	____	____	____	____	____	____	____	______	____
Community	____	____	____	____	____	____	____	______	____
Business	____	____	____	____	____	____	____	______	____
Recreation	____	____	____	____	____	____	____	______	____
Misc	____	____	____	____	____	____	____	______	____
							Home subtotal	______	____

Work

Unscheduled visitors (pleasure) ____ ____ ____ ____ ____ ____ ____ ______ ____

Unscheduled visitors (business) ____ ____ ____ ____ ____ ____ ____ ______ ____

Scheduled visitors (pleasure) ____ ____ ____ ____ ____ ____ ____ ______ ____

Scheduled visitors (business) ____ ____ ____ ____ ____ ____ ____ ______ ____

Visitors subtotal ______ ____

Outgoing telephone (pleasure) ____ ____ ____ ____ ____ ____ ____ ______ ____

Outgoing telephone (business) ____ ____ ____ ____ ____ ____ ____ ______ ____

Incoming telephone (personal) ____ ____ ____ ____ ____ ____ ____ ______ ____

Incoming telephone (business) ____ ____ ____ ____ ____ ____ ____ ______ ____

Telephone subtotal ______ ____

Group meetings ____ ____ ____ ____ ____ ____ ____ ______ ____

Waiting ____ ____ ____ ____ ____ ____ ____ ______ ____

Breaks ____ ____ ____ ____ ____ ____ ____ ______ ____

Reading ____ ____ ____ ____ ____ ____ ____ ______ ____

Writing ____ ____ ____ ____ ____ ____ ____ ______ ____

Faxing ____ ____ ____ ____ ____ ____ ____ ______ ____

Planning ____ ____ ____ ____ ____ ____ ____ ______ ____

Physical work ____ ____ ____ ____ ____ ____ ____ ______ ____

Misc ____ ____ ____ ____ ____ ____ ____ ______ ____

Total of all categories ______ ____

After categorising and recording your time log information, determine which time expenditures you wish to change. To do this, you'll need to ask some pertinent questions, including:

1. Did I use any time to plan for the future?

2. Have I recorded activity – or results? (Activity = what I did. Results = what I accomplished.)

3. What was the longest period spent on one thing without interruption?

4. Which interruptions were most costly?

5. What can be done to eliminate or control these interruptions?
   - Which telephone calls were unnecessary?
   - Which phone calls could have been shorter yet equally (or more) effective?
   - Which visits were unnecessary?
   - Which visits could have been shorter yet equally (or more) effective?

6. How much time was spent in meetings?
   - How much was necessary?
   - How could more have been accomplished in less time?

7. Did I find myself jumping from task to task without completing the previous one?

8. Did urgent or crisis work push other things aside?

9. Did I notice a self-correcting tendency occurring as I recorded actions throughout the week?

When you have answered these questions, you are in a much better position to decide what you must change in order to save time in your work and personal life. Of course, you may discover that what you do is exactly what you want to do; if so, your final decision will be to do nothing. In either case, the information will help you to make the right decision.

And if you make changes, be aware of two points:

1. Increasing the amount of time spent on one activity will require that you take time from another activity.
2. Changes can sometimes cause problems which in turn take even more time to remedy.

What is 'Urgent'?

Dr Charles Hummel once wrote an article entitled 'The Tyranny of the Urgent'. In it he distinguished things that are truly important from those that seem 'urgent'. When important things and urgent things occur at the same time, which usually wins our attention? Let me give you an example.

A number of years ago, I made the decision to leave the organisation I worked for in London and move my family back to my home town. I planned to be my own boss, as an independent training consultant. After a couple of grim years, I finally achieved my bottom line financial goal – ie, we weren't starving!

At the time, my office was in our converted garage. We had several children so I decided to have a business telephone line and a family line.

One Friday evening at about 5.30 we were sitting down to supper when the business line rang. I asked the children to quieten down, and answered the phone. 'International Training Consultants – Dick Leatherman speaking. How can I help you?' I said.

The caller was the course director of a local management centre. He was extremely agitated – so much so that I could hardly understand him. I was also being distracted by noise in the kitchen, so I put him on hold and went down to the garage to continue the call. 'What's wrong?' I asked.

His story was a course director's nightmare. He was at the end of a week-long seminar for about a hundred buyers from up and down the country. The key speaker for Saturday morning was the dean of one of the country's leading law faculties. But unfortunately he had just gone down with the flu and couldn't be there in the morning.

So the course director pleaded, 'Dick, will you be our key speaker tomorrow morning? We don't care what you do. Just come in and do something!' As you can imagine the request made me feel good. I was the first person he had called!

But let's put him on hold for a minute so I can tell you about several things I had already arranged for the Saturday in question.

First, because my office was at home we had some pretty strict rules about the children bothering me when I was working. A week before the course director's call, I had been working in my office when Matthew Leatherman (he was about seven years old at the time) barged in with a big emergency. Well, he wasn't broken or bleeding, and I was irritated that he had interrupted me. As a result I wasn't very nice to him. And as he sulked out of my office, he said under his breath (but just loud enough for me to hear him), 'Daddy doesn't have time for me any more now he has his own business.' And Matthew was right. I wasn't spending as much time with him as I once did.

So I said, 'Hang on a second. You're right. I don't spend as much time with you as I used to. But I'll tell you what – why don't we have a rabbit day next Saturday morning. 'Would you like that?' 'Oh, yes!' he exclaimed, and I got a big hug.

Do you know what a 'rabbit day' is? It's when you take a seven-year old boy out to look for rabbits. The fact that you probably won't find any is not the point. It's what you can talk about while you look! One-to-one private chats between a father and his son. That's the point!

And there was another important thing I had arranged for that Saturday. Laurie, my 16-year-old (going on 21), had asked me the preceding Wednesday if I would teach her how to drive. I said, 'Hey, I don't want to pay for your professional driving lessons and still end up teaching you myself! Besides, you don't want to learn my bad driving habits.' (I'm an awful driver.)

'But Daddy,' she replied, 'I've never driven a car, and I've got my first lesson next week. The other girls will be there too, and I don't want to make a fool of myself in front of them!' 'Oh, I see,' I said. 'I'll tell you what – let's spend some time next Saturday at the derelict airfield, and you can scare me to death!' 'Fantastic!' she said. And I got a big hug for that, too.

The last thing I had arranged for that Saturday was some time with my youngest daughter, Leanne. Her 'Uncle Frank' had made her a giant doll's house. It was amazing! It was carpeted, and had real windows. It also had a low-voltage lighting system with a miniature chandelier hanging in the dining room.

Well, Leanne's house had an attic fire. Somehow the low-voltage wiring had shorted and the transformer had burned out. She had been 'reminding' me to fix if for a couple of months. And the Tuesday before the Saturday in question, she had asked, 'Please, please, please, (or were there four 'pleases'?) fix my doll's house?' I said 'I'll tell you what I'm going to do. I'll put the transformer in your doll's house this coming Saturday. At the same time, I'll teach you how to solder wires.' I got another big hug for that!

Remember, we still have the course director on 'hold'. What do you think I told him when he frantically said that Friday, 'Dick, we don't care what you do. Just come in and do something!' Yes – I said 'Okay.'

Then I walked into the kitchen and said, 'Guess what, Daddy has a seminar at the management centre tomorrow morning!' There was dead silence. Then my oldest daughter said, 'Daddy!'

and walked out of the room. Matthew said, 'But . . . but . . . what about rabbit day?' And Leanne, with all the faith and trust of a young child in her father, said, 'That's all right, Daddy. I know you'll fix my doll's house some day.'

I did eventually fix the doll's house, go rabbit searching with Matthew, and give Laurie some hints on driving. But not that day – when I let the urgent win over those things that were truly important to me.

Two lessons can be learned from my experience. First, there is no end to it: the 'tyranny of the urgent' is a battle we all fight day after day. Do you imagine this was the last time I let a crisis get in the way of something that was really important? The thing we must try to do at home and at work is to choose well when the 'urgent' tries to displace the truly *important*.

Second, as Peter Drucker has said, 'Learn to say "no", nicely if you can but nastily if you must. But learn to say "no", so that you have time for the really important things in your life.'

If saying no is difficult for you, recognise that you can't say yes to everything. In other words, you have a right to say no. A simple, 'No, thank you' is often sufficient and appropriate for those situations where a personal relationship with the other individual is not at issue. And sometimes you will have to say no more than once. Here's an example.

It is 6.30pm and you are in the middle of eating supper. The phone rings and you answer it, 'Hello?'

Caller: 'Is that Ms Brown?'

You: 'Yes.'

Caller: 'Wonderful! This is William Appleby from the Easy Glide Home Appliance Company. I am happy to inform you that you have won a matching set of stainless steel kitchen knives with genuine wooden handles. One of our representatives will be in your area next week to deliver your prize. When would it be convenient for her to call?'

You: 'Thank you, but I'm really not interested.'

Caller: 'Ms Brown, our computer selected you at random for this free set of superb knives that I know you will love having in your home. It won't take a minute to have them delivered to you. So which would be the best time for you, Monday or Tuesday of next week?'

You: 'Thank you, but I'm really not interested.'

Caller: 'I'm sorry, but I don't understand. Why aren't you interested in owning this free set of fantastic knives?'

You: 'Thank you, but I'm really not interested.'

At this point, if the caller continues to be a pest, say, 'Thank you for calling. Goodbye' – and hang up.

But if a personal relationship with the other person is important to you, first acknowledge the request, then say no, and last add an explanation. For example, suppose you are a great typist. You have a good friend who is taking evening classes at the local college. The conversation goes as follows:

Friend: 'Do you have a minute?'

You: 'Of course, Sarah. What's up?'

Friend: 'I really hate to ask you, but I've got a special paper that I have to hand in on Friday. I can't find anybody who can type it for me. Would you mind doing it?'

You: 'It sounds like you're facing a tight deadline. I'd really like to help you but I can't. I don't have time to do it.

Friend: 'I know you are busy, and I really hate to ask you. But you type so fast using your word processor. It's only ten pages. Isn't there some way you could squeeze it in?'

You: 'I'm really sorry Sarah, but I can't. I have other plans.'

Note that you acknowledged her needs ('It sounds like you're facing a tight deadline'), said no tactfully ('I'd really like to help you but I can't'), and gave a reason ('I don't have time to do it'). Note, too, that when your friend persisted in her request, you said no again.

But how do you know when to say no? By realising what is important to you. And how do you ensure that important things are not pushed aside by 'urgent' things?

By planning! Planning allows you to identify important goals, and put them into action. The resulting activities generated by this analysis then become a part of your daily planning.

Daily planning

Daily planning is making a 'to-do' list for each day. This list should include the priority items that need to be accomplished immediately, as well as things that you can do today to help carry out your long-range goals. It doesn't have to be anything fancy – just a small piece of paper you carry in your pocket or handbag to jot down the things you have planned for that (or the next) day. It doesn't make any difference when you do it, whether first thing in the morning or at the end of the day. Just as long as you do it daily!

But keeping a to-do list on a daily basis may involve a significant amount of time. For example, even if you spend only 10 minutes a day making your list, that adds up to about 2400 minutes – 40 hours – a year! So there is a cost for making a daily to-do list. And thus there must be a compelling reason to lead you to do such daily planning.

In fact, there are a number of good reasons why effective people do daily planning. First, when all the things you feel you need to do today are visibly identified, you can establish your priorities by seeing what's important, and what's only urgent.

Daily planning also helps your supervisor or manager to set priorities with you. For example, if your supervisor or manager constantly interrupts you with new crisis requests, it's strategically helpful to be able to hold up a daily to-do list and say, 'All right, boss, where does that fit in on my list?'

Third, a to-do list acts as a memory aid. I, for one, have reached an age where if I don't write it down, there is only a very small chance I'll remember what it was that I said I absolutely wouldn't forget!

I use a daily to-do list for yet another reason. It tells me what to do next after finishing a task. I am a very task-orientated person. While I'm working on a task, I usually don't think of other things that need to be done. Then when I finish a job, because I can't think of what I wanted to do next, I may simply take a break. But if I have a to-do list in front of me, I can see exactly what I need to do next.

Others who keep daily to-do lists say that it simply feels good to tick tasks off their lists as they are completed. In other words, you have set up a way of giving yourself immediate positive feedback as each task is finished.

Finally, I save my lists for a month or so and review them to see if I can discover any ways that I can further improve my time management. For example, if I haven't completed a task that I had planned to do that day, I immediately rewrite that task on the next day's list. And if I see that I carried over a particular task more than once, I realise that I may be putting it off.

If you don't now use a daily to-do list, try it! It will be time well invested. Or simply commit yourself to keeping a list for 20 working days. When you see that it pays off, you will continue to use such a list naturally because you've become used to the 'to-do habit'.

One example of a to-do list is given below. Draft your own version and make as many copies as you need and then cut the paper into quarters. Stack the quarter sheets and staple at the top to make your own to-do pads.

Summary

We have presented several concrete strategies for managing your time well:

- Time logs
- Prioritising important things over 'urgent' ones
- Daily planning with 'to-do lists'

Using these techniques will allow you to accomplish key tasks on time – and give you more time for creative thinking, for your boss and for yourself. To become a better manager of your time, you need to spend it on those things that are really important. In short, you need to take control of your life!

MANAGING YOUR TIME
To-do list

Tasks to do	Priority	Time

Chapter 10

Managing Your Performance Appraisal

Some years ago I had a boss who was truly incompetent in conducting performance appraisals. To compound the problem, he had no idea that he didn't know how to handle employee appraisal meetings. The result of his brief, once-a-year session was that I resented him and felt badly towards the organisation I worked for. And most importantly, I felt bad about myself.

But I knew that his short annual presentation of my strengths and weaknesses was a poor way to conduct a performance appraisal. Since that time, I have read everything I could on the topic of performance appraisal. I have also attended numerous workshops on this subject, conducted appraisal sessions with many employees, talked to thousands of managers, supervisors, and employees, and taught hundreds of workshops on this topic.

And only now, some 35 years after my first unfortunate experiences, do I feel comfortable - most of the time - participating in a performance appraisal session. I have learned a lot, and much of it the hard way!

What's in this section Following is a step-by-step approach for you to use in *managing* your performance appraisal interviews. This planned approach will help you to provide your supervisor or manager with better information to help him or her conduct a productive, balanced, and fair performance appraisal session with you.

This method is *not* a 'sit-back-and-listen-as-your-boss-tells-you-your-strengths-and-weaknesses' approach. It is *participative*. But there is a cost to you. It requires that you spend time preparing for your meeting. You will find, as a result, that the appraisal interview will run longer - to your advantage. There may also be more open disagreements during your meeting. But an open discussion will allow you and your leader to arrive at a true understanding of your actual performance.

Planning for the review

Sometimes we run into problems in our performance appraisal interviews because we don't know clearly what is expected of us. 'I didn't know I was supposed to do that!' many of us have said. In addition, most of us have asked questions, such as, 'What is a good job?' or 'When am I not doing this job well enough?' And 'When am I devoting too much time and energy to this task?' These questions indicate that someone hasn't explained what is expected of us during the period being appraised.

Analysing your job

To avoid such problems, plan a meeting with your boss 6 to 12 months ahead to discuss your specific job responsibilities. By making copies of and filling in the following job analysis work sheet, you will be prepared to discuss and obtain agreement on your job tasks with your supervisor or manager.

Job analysis work sheet

List the main tasks of your job	How critical is each job task? A = Highest B = Medium C = Lowest	What standards are used to measure your job performance?	What problems exist which handicap your performance?	Authority levels*		
				1	2	3

*A '1 authority level' means that you, the employee, have total authority to perform the task. In other words, you don't have to ask permission to do the task or even tell your boss that you did it. You simply do it because it's a routine part of your job. A '2 authority level' allows you to perform the task without first asking permission. But you are expected to let your boss know that you did it. A '3 authority level' indicates that you need to obtain approval from your boss before doing that task.

Fill in the work sheet. Then discuss it with your manager. You are likely to be amazed at the number of times the two of you do not agree about which tasks are most important, the standards for tasks and the authority you have for each task. And you will find that this meeting will help greatly to ensure that your efforts are on track. Your next performance appraisal meetings will be more fair and productive as a result.

Reminder file

It will also be helpful for you to keep a performance appraisal reminder file throughout the year. When you complete a special project or do a job well, make a note of this and place it in your file. Similarly, when you have problems with a task, work out what happened and write it up for your file. Then when you are preparing for your next performance appraisal session, you will have accurate information to use in doing a candid self-assessment. (See the interview form found at the end of this chapter.)

Preparing for the performance appraisal interview

An effective performance appraisal interview requires that you and your supervisor spend time talking about your past performance, areas for improvement and ways to make your strengths even better. Too often this does not happen. If such a discussion is important to you, you may need to take the initiative to prepare yourself for the interview.

The organisation's system

If your organisation has a poor appraisal system, you may have difficulty changing it. But there *are* important things you can do – things that will not only help you to receive a fair and constructive appraisal interview, but will also help your boss and the organisation as well.

For example, suppose your organisation expects your supervisor to present you with your completed appraisal, giving you little or no opportunity for input. An effective way of solving this problem is to ask your boss to conduct an informal appraisal interview with you every three months, as well as shortly *before* the 'official' appraisal session. This will not only produce an interview that is fairer to you, but will you give your boss better information to use when he or she is later required to fill in the appraisal form.

If your boss feels a need to stay with an out-of-date company policy regulation that requires that you simply be presented with your appraisal, then don't count this as an 'informal performance appraisal meeting'. Simply label it something else. Most leaders, for example, will be happy to schedule a private meeting with you in order to 'review your job performance'.

On the other hand, suppose that your organisation's performance appraisal system is good, but your supervisor's approach isn't. For example, if your boss spent only a few minutes conducting your last appraisal interview, the first thing you need to do is to let him or her know ahead of time that you are preparing in advance for your next interview, and would appreciate at least an hour of uninterrupted time for it.

Your responsibility

Next, prepare carefully. If you don't have a copy of the performance appraisal form that your organisation uses, find one. Then look it over to become familiar with its layout. Assess the kinds of information requested. Most appraisal forms list general duties, personality traits and work habits, and rate you on them. Other forms are customised for your specific job, and ratings are assigned for each of your major job duties. (This is the better type of form.)

Whatever kind of form your organisation uses, it will normally ask the rater to analyse your strengths and the areas which need improvement. This is where you will be doing most of your preparation. The idea is for *you* to be thoroughly prepared to discuss both your strengths and weaknesses. And if you have a participative supervisor, he or she will appreciate your preparation because it will make his or her job that much easier.

One word of caution. It is best not to plan to discuss salary, promotion or your career path in this meeting. It is very difficult to discuss honestly your past, present and future performance if, at the same time, you are looking for a promotion or salary increase. It is far better to concentrate on your performance at this meeting and set up another meeting at a later time to discuss a salary increase or promotion.

What you do

Here are the steps to follow in preparing for your performance appraisal interview:

1. If you don't know the date of your next appraisal interview, find out. Otherwise you may find yourself surprised by your boss walking up to your desk and saying, 'I'd like to see you in my office at ten o'clock this morning for your annual performance appraisal interview.' You need to learn when your interview is scheduled so that you will have sufficient time to prepare for it. If you aren't given an exact date, try to determine an approximate one.
2. If you don't have a blank copy of your organisation's performance appraisal form (or a copy of your appraisal the previous year), get one and look it over. Don't fill it in at this point. Simply review it to determine what information is needed.
3. Next, list the major duties of your job and evaluate the tasks that represent your strengths and the areas where you need to improve.
4. Look at each of your job strengths to see if there is any way this skill could be even further developed. Also, look to see if any of your strengths are not being fully used by your organisation at the present time. If this is so, develop any strategies that will better match your strengths to the needs of your department or section.
5. Then examine the job areas where you feel your performance needs to be improved. Your first task is to analyse, for each need area, *why* unsatisfactory results are occurring (or satisfactory results are not occurring). When you feel you understand the causes of any problems, try to develop possible solutions.
6. If your organisation's performance appraisal form requires noting personality traits and/or job habits, be sure also to analyse them in order to determine your strengths and needs. Although these may not be directly related to job performance, improvements in job habits and/or personality traits often help us to become more effective.
7. Write out brief action plans for improving your performance in the areas of both your strengths and needs. These action plans will be tentative at this point, since you will be asking your boss later for his or her evaluation and ideas for improving them.
8. Now, using the information from Steps 3 to 7, fill in the form yourself. This will help you to prepare by allowing you to see better how your boss may approach your meeting, and how he or she may perceive you.
9. If you know that your organisation's performance appraisal

system will not allow you to provide input during the actual interview, then ask your supervisor for a one-hour private meeting to informally discuss your 'job performance'. If your boss normally conducts such interviews in his or her office, where interruptions are a problem, ask if he or she would be willing to reserve a conference room or some other location where you can have privacy.

Then the day before this job performance meeting, remind your boss that it has been arranged for the next day and that you are looking forward to it. (Supervisors and managers, like others, sometimes forget meetings that they didn't initiate.)

Managing your performance appraisal interview

Your goal in your performance appraisal interview is to actively guide the discussion along the most helpful channels without being offensive. If you do all the talking, you will not be able to take advantage of your boss's suggestions, ideas and advice. On the other hand, if you allow your boss to do all the talking, he or she will not have the opportunity to learn important things from and about you. The best strategy is to maintain a balance between these two extremes. In a particular performance appraisal session, a good guideline might be for you to talk about 60 per cent of the time and your supervisor or manager about 40 per cent.

Please note that the step-by-step plan that follows requires that you be honest - honest with yourself and honest with your boss. You will find it fairly easy to be honest when discussing your strengths. But it may be a lot harder to maintain equal honesty when discussing areas in which you need to improve!

It is important for you to come clean with your boss in discussing areas of needed improvement. For one thing, if you present only your strengths, you will lose control of the interview when your boss brings your 'weaknesses' up for discussion. It is far better for you to present your areas of need than to make your boss do so because you have not.

Second, if you don't bring up problem areas for discussion, you communicate that you don't feel confident about how your boss will react. Also, you will not appear to have an objective view of yourself (we can all improve), or the capacity for self-criticism needed for growth. And if you don't bring up problem areas, and your boss also fails to do so, how are you going to get ideas for improvement?

A good balance between speaking and listening, with honesty, is not easy to attain – especially without a plan. But with a well-conceived step-by-step approach you can achieve this balance.

Step-by-step approach

The following outline will help you to manage your performance appraisal interview with fair, constructive, and profitable results for all concerned.

1. Introduction.

   Greet your supervisor or manager and tell him or her how pleased you are to have this opportunity to meet and discuss your performance. Thank him or her for the uninterrupted time that has been set aside for the meeting, and also for the time that he or she may have spent in preparation.

2. Agree to the objectives for this meeting.

   Ask your manager or supervisor what he or she considers the major objectives for this meeting.

   Next ask if you could first:

   - present your thoughts on your strengths and achievements
   - present your view of areas where you need additional improvement
   - discuss your tentative action plans for improving your performance in specific areas
   - secure his or her reaction, ideas and suggestions about these plans.

   Then ask if he or she would help you to:

   - gain further feedback on the areas of strength and the need that you did not mention
   - obtain help in setting priorities on the things that need to be done as a result of the meeting.

3. Present your topics for discussion.

- First, present one of your strengths.
  — Describing the strength, using specific examples.

Example: Don't simply state, 'First, I'd like to mention my success in organising my work.'
Better to say, 'First, I'd like to discuss my ability to organise my work. For example, several months ago, I spent a lot of time analysing my work flow. Based on that analysis I established a new system of prioritising each job I receive. This has helped to reduce the amount of time I have had to spend on 'fire-fighting', and has allowed me to manage my work much more productively.'

- Next, present your tentative action plan for using this strength even better.

Example: You might say, 'Here are some ideas I have on how I can further organise my work.'

- Then solicit ideas for better use of this strength.

Example: 'What suggestions do you have for using my organisational ability to even better advantage?'

Or, 'How can I be even more productive in this area?'

- Finally, discuss any ideas that have emerged, and arrive at an agreement.

Follow this format in discussing other important areas of strength. However, because of time constraints it would be wise to select only a few of your major strengths for this initial meeting.

- Next, identify an area of work where you wish to improve your performance.
  — Describe what is happening in this area in specific terms. Use examples to illustrate the problem if possible.

Example: 'I find that I am constantly interrupted. Some of the interruptions are related to my job, but some aren't. As a result, I find that I don't get as much done as I would like. During the past week, for example, I kept an "interruption list". By the end of the week, I found that I had been interrupted an average of 11 times per day and only about 40 per cent of the interruptions were work-related.'

— Describe what you want to happen. Again, be specific, avoiding general statements if possible.

Example: 'I am not sure what is "normal". But I think if I could reduce the non-work-related interruptions by at least 50 per cent, I could be a lot more effective.'

• State what you feel is the cause (or causes) of the problem.

Example: 'I studied my log to see if I could find any patterns. And interestingly enough, I saw that one individual accounted for an average of two interruptions per day. And there were at least two other interruptions a day from people who wanted to borrow items from me. So I see two causes. One cause is an employee who likes to talk, and I don't say no. And the other cause concerns my desk. My desk seems to be the local supply cabinet! I was interrupted twice for aspirin, and once for a pencil sharpener. Someone else needed to borrow my extra stamp pad, another person wanted a red pen, and a third person asked for a bright green highlighter pen.'

— Describe your suggested solution(s).

Example: 'As I see it, there are two things I can do. First is to stop being the local supply cabinet. I'll clear out my desk, put extra supplies back in the supply cupboard and let everybody know what I've done.'
'Dealing with the individual who is interrupting me will be more difficult. She is going through a separation from her husband and needs to talk to somebody – and it looks as though I've been

elected! I want to help by being there for her, but it is becoming a major problem for me. What I would like to do is be straight with her about my job needs and suggest we meet for lunch or chat at break times. What I don't want to do is make her think that nobody cares.'

— Describe your tentative action plan.

(In the example above, it is probably not necessary to have a detailed action plan, since most of the solutions seem to be fairly obvious.)

— Ask for feedback on your plans, and additional suggestions.

Example: 'What do you think?' or 'What other ideas do you have?'

— Discuss suggestions and arrive at a consensus.

— Present any other important areas of needed improvement following the same format. Again, due to time limitations, you may wish to select only a few key areas to discuss.

4. Request information about areas of strength or need that you have not already mentioned.

   - Ask: 'What other strengths or areas where improvement is needed do you feel we should discuss that I haven't mentioned?'

Here, it is very important that you not become defensive when your boss brings up an area, where he or she feels you need to improve. It may be difficult – but listen; don't interrupt. Don't mentally prepare your response. Instead, ask questions. Ask for examples to help your supervisor or manager explain his or her viewpoint. Again do not become upset about seemingly 'negative' feedback. You are not being attacked! Remember that your boss is trying to help you by offering suggestions for improvements – which you have just asked for.

5. Prioritise the topics that have been discussed.

   If a number of different strengths and areas for improvement have been discussed, it may be necessary to prioritise them, for two reasons. First, implementing new solutions and plans will require a significant amount of time. But you may not have enough time to handle all the needed changes immediately. Second, you and your supervisor or manager may need to agree on which action plan is most important - which one should be implemented first.

6. Establish dates for a follow-up meeting.

   In your follow-up meeting, you will discuss the progress you have made in implementing your plan(s) for improvement, and discuss any additional problems that may be occurring as a result of the changes you have made.

7. Thank your supervisor or manager for his or her time and suggestions.

A planning work sheet that uses this approach is shown on the following pages. It will help you to outline the steps you will need to follow in your performance appraisal review. The experience of many employees and supervisors indicates that this time-tested approach will prove to be both productive and rewarding.

Managing your performance appraisal interview
Work sheet

Write below what you plan to say during the interview. Do not write a word-for-word 'script', just your notes indicating what you want to say at each step of the interview,

1. **Introduction**
   Greeting: ______________________________
   ____
   Express your appreciation: ______________________________
   ____

2. **Agree to the objectives for this meeting**
   ____
   ____
   ____
   ____
   ____

3. **Present your topics for discussion**
   A. Describe a key strength: ______________________________
   ____
   Example(s) of this strength: ______________________________
   ____
   Present your tentative action plan for even better use of this strength (if applicable): ______________________________
   ____
   ____
   ____
   ____
   ____
   ____
   Solicit ideas for greater use of this strength. Write the question you will ask: ______________________________
   ____
   Record suggested ideas: ______________________________
   ____
   ____
   ____
   ____
   ____

Discuss suggestions, and arrive at a consensus.
Record your agreement: ______________________________
____
____
____
____

If you have more than one strength to present, duplicate these pages and continue this step until completed.

B. Present for discussion an area of your work in which you feel you need to improve your performance.
Described what has been happening, in specific terms:
____
____
____
____

Note examples: ______________________________________
____
____

Describe what you want to happen. Again, be specific:
____
____
____
____

State what you think is the cause (or causes) of the problem:
____
____
____
____

Describe your suggested solution(s):
____
____
____
____

Describe any tentative action plan(s) you may have:
____
____
____
____
____
____

Ask for feedback on your plan(s) and additional suggestions. Indicate the question you will ask: ______

______

Record reactions and suggestions: ______

______

______

______

Discuss suggestions and arrive at consensus. Record your agreement: ______

______

______

If you have more than one improvement to present, duplicate these pages and continue this step until completed.

4. **Request additional information about areas of strength or need for improvement that you have not already mentioned**

Indicate question you will ask: ______

______

______

Note strengths that are mentioned (with suggestions for making even better use of them, if they are given): ______

______

______

Note areas needing improvement if they are mentioned: ______

______

______

______

What examples illustrate this concern? ______

______

______

______

How should you be performing? ______

______

______

______

What does your manager feel is the cause of the situation?

______

______

What do you feel is the cause of the situation? ______

______

What solutions or suggestions does your manager have? _____

____

____

What other solutions do you see? ___________________________

____

____

Describe your action plan(s) below:

____

____

____

____

____

____

____

____

____

Make several copies of these pages to take with you into the interview (ie, one for each area of improvement that might be suggested).

5. **Prioritise the topics that have been discussed**
   List below (on one line if possible) each of the topics discussed during the meeting:

Topic	Priority

Looking over the above topics with your manager, jointly assign priorities to those topics (areas for improvement, strengths) that need follow-up action. (ie, which should be addressed first, which second, and so on. Or which is most important, next most important, etc).

6. **Establish dates for a follow-up meeting**
   Indicate how you will ask for a follow-up meeting: ____________
   ____
   When would be a good time for you? ____________________
   Tentative follow-up date: __________________________

7. **Thank your supervisor or manager for his or her time and suggestions**
   Indicate what you will say: _________________________
   ____
   ____
   ____
   ____
   ____
   ____
   ____
   ____
   ____
   ____
   ____
   ____
   ____
   ____
   ____
   ____
   ____

Chapter 11

It's *Your* Career

In the preceding chapters, I have made a strong case for the need to accept personal responsibility in managing your performance appraisal interview, your time, your attitude – each part of your working life. And this is also true in managing your career development. Your organisation is not responsible for your career. Your boss is not responsible for your career. You are!

Developing a career plan, either with the help of your organisation or on your own, can help you to overcome obstacles and achieve success

Career development systems

Good organisations know that their employees are their strength. Today you will find such organisations helping employees to build careers to become more and more valuable to the organisation. As you can see from the diagram of the way the parts of a modern career system fit together, the central focus is on career counselling and career action plans.

Organisational strategies

Organisations are built on a foundation of strategic planning. This planning is usually conducted by top management in order to define the organisation's mission or vision. From the organisation's definition of what it is about – its vision and mission – a long-range plan is developed.

After the organisation does long-range planning, it can forecast its human resource needs. When the forecasting is complete, the organisation can do succession planning to determine who needs to be trained to do what in future jobs. Then the organisation communicates its human resource needs to its employees by job allocation.

But even if your organisation does not do forecasting or succession planning, you can still take responsibility for your career development. The first step for you is to work out where you are

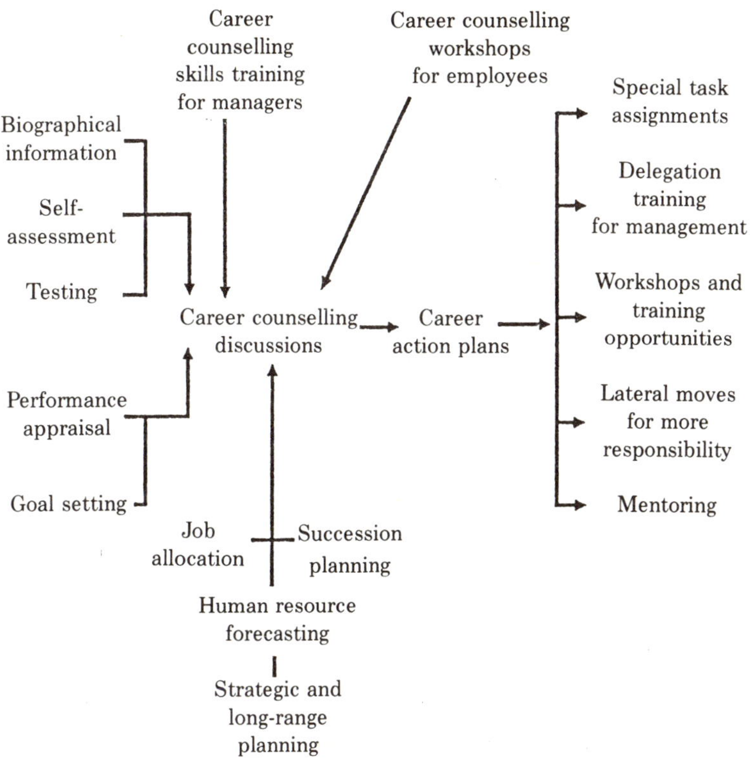

going, what knowledge and skills will be required, and then determine what you need to do to get there.

Useful strategies for determining your needs

To explore your developmental needs, you will need to analyse your past experiences to determine your strengths, knowledge, skills and values. This information will be very useful to you and your supervisor or manager in helping you to make a sound career development decisions.

For example, if you looked at my background you would discover that in almost every job I have had, I've enjoyed making presentations. Even in high school, my only A was in Public Speaking. Therefore, if you were assisting me with my career planning, you would focus on my strength of being able to make presentations.

Job history form.
One way to organise information about yourself is to fill in a 'job history' form. To fill in a copy of this form (found at the end of this chapter), begin by listing each job you have held in the past, starting with your present job (maximum of five). A major job change within one organisation is counted as a new job.

Next, break each job down into tasks. Enter the details on the form. Then show your personal level of satisfaction for each task. Finally, for those tasks rated highest or lowest in satisfaction, note the reasons why you liked or disliked each task. This list will provide themes and clues to the key things you want in a career, as well as the things you wish to avoid.

The following is an example of a job history for one of my past positions:

Job history

1. Job	**2. Major tasks**	**3. Satisfaction** 5 = High level 1 = Low level	**4. Why did you like or dislike this specific task?**
Department	Team leader	3	
Manager	Long-range planning	4	
	Handling budgets	1	I hate dealing with budgets because I am not very good at it!
	Writing and creating new courses	3	
	Making presentations to executives	2	
	Acting as resource person for technical questions	5	I enjoy being the 'expert' and helping people.
	Speaking at local and national conventions	5	The recognition I receive feels good to me. I also like being competent.

5. What generalisations (themes) can you make about yourself from your job history analysis? What are the key things you want in a job, and what do you wish to avoid?

1. I like the mentoring role. ______________________________

____

2. Recognition for work well done is important to me. ______

____

3. I would strongly dislike working with numbers. __________

____

Life history form.
In addition to the job history form, you should also fill in a copy of a 'life history' form (found at the end of this chapter). This form also asks you to identify major skills and interests.

To use this form, first list five key positive events that have occurred in your life, either job-related or personal, that resulted mostly from your own efforts. Then, for each event list the skills or abilities you used that produced the positive experience.

Next, honestly indicate specific reasons why each of the events was important to you. Then examine each of your skills and abilities and make a new list of the most important ones. Finally, as a result of analysing the reasons why each positive event was personally important, list the underlying values that were shown in that event. That is, list what you liked and enjoyed about each situation.

To illustrate the use of this form, take as an example a life event that was significant for me. The teachers in my primary school thought I was 'strange'. I could read at an astonishing speed. But I could not spell.

It wasn't until I was in further education that I learned I had a condition referred to as 'dyslexia'. Many years later I felt honoured to be asked to give an address to a special school sixth form class of 12 students – who were all dyslexic! The life history form overleaf shows how I addressed this positive event.

It is difficult to perceive the power of these two forms until you have had an opportunity to use them. At the end of this chapter there is a set of both forms to copy and fill in for yourself.

Life history

1. Positive event	2. List your skills/abilities that resulted in this event	3. Why was this event important to you?
I gave an opening address to a sixth form class of dyslexics	– Speaking before groups – Writing skills (not spelling!) – Knowledge of how to conduct a needs assessment (I interviewed each of the 12 students before writing the speech)	– Recognition; I felt needed – Satisfaction in helping others personally

4. From 2 above, list your most important skills and abilities	5. Identify your underlying values
Speaking before groups	– I like being in a situation where I can help others and be perceived as being exceptional – I enjoy the resulting recognition

Testing

There are a number of tests or questionnaires that can help you to determine your career interests or needs. Examples of such tests are John Holland's *Self-Directed Search*, the Myers-Briggs *Type Indicator*, and for supervisory or management positions, the *Leatherman Leadership Questionnaire*. Tests such as these can usually be obtained from your organisation's personnel department.

There are two main kinds of test to help people determine career interests and needs. The more common tests are called 'perception' questionnaires. 'Knowledge-based' questionnaires are less common.

Perception questionnaires

These tests are used to determine which of a list of topics are perceived as being career development needs. For example, a questionnaire that begins by asking an employee, 'Which of the following topics do you feel are important for your future development?' belongs in this class of test.

Perception tests are easy and quick to complete. They can be filled in by the person being tested, the boss or a peer.

Unfortunately, perception tests also have very serious limitations. For example, some topics from a career development test may be selected as critical when, in fact, they may not be needs at all. If topics such as 'communication' or 'time management' appear in a list, they are almost guaranteed to be selected as critical. This is because they are what we call umbrella terms.

In other words, terms like 'communication', and 'time management' are labels that cover a number of different subtopics. If any subparts are really important to you, you will mark 'time management' as important. But other parts may not be important to you at all.

Also, what people think they need, and what they really need, may be quite different. For example, you may have little competence in managing your performance appraisal interviews and not know that you need help in this area. This often happens when your supervisor or manager doesn't know how to interview either. In fact, entire organisations often don't know that they don't know how to conduct performance appraisals effectively!

Knowledge-based questionnaires

These tests, on the other hand, are used to determine our actual knowledge in specific areas. For example, a typical knowledge-based question would resemble the following:

The primary responsibility for career development rests with the:

A. Employee's immediate supervisor.
B. Personnel department's establishment of career development paths and procedures (eg, mentoring, training courses, career planning systems).
C. Employee.
D. Chief executive of the organisation, since his or her support is essential for the success of any career development path.

Like perception tests, knowledge-based tests are easy to administer. But unlike perception tests, knowledge-based tests provide very accurate information if they are properly developed. Also, they show exactly what the person knows, rather than what he or she thinks.

Assessment centres

Another testing strategy that is used by some large organisations to determine career development needs is called an 'assessment centre'. An assessment centre uses a several-day process with trained observers to rate employees as they complete a variety of simulated tasks.

For example, each assessor observes participants for one to five days as they participate in group discussions, work individually on special assignments, give presentations, solve problems, and make decisions.

Assessment centres have proved to be a valid and reliable way of discovering employee developmental needs. In addition, the feedback given to the employees at the end of the assessment period is usually quite helpful.

But assessment centres place heavy stress on the people tested. And they cost a lot to run, even though they test only small groups of people.

Performance appraisal systems

Another source that can help to identify your needs and strengths is a performance appraisal – when it is done properly (see Chapter 10). If your boss is honest and accurate in his or her feedback to you, if the appraisal system is designed to allow you to be a part of the discussion, and if the performance appraisal form includes information about your future, then good career development information can be obtained.

But for the performance appraisal interview to be worthwhile for you – and the organisation – you must have an opportunity well in advance to discuss your job responsibilities with your supervisor or manager (as much as one year prior to the interview, if possible). This type of interview is important in order to reduce the chances that you will later be appraised on things you should have done but didn't. Here there should be a full discussion of the job's tasks, the standards for each task, your authority level for the task, and a careful analysis of any problems that might impede your performance.

In addition, your manager or supervisor must be able to give you honest and straightforward feedback in appraising you. Managers and supervisors must also be willing to spend time in the appraisal interview discussing not only your past and present performance, but your future as well. And last, the performance appraisal form itself should address such issues as career planning and setting future developmental goals and objectives.

As a part of a complete performance management system, some organisations use a formal goal-setting process where you, with your leader's help, write job-related goals and objectives, and then create a plan to reach each objective. This type of information, even though it is aimed at your present job tasks, can provide further career development data.

Career development workshops

Most performance appraisal systems fall short of the desired standard. Therefore, many organisations have helped the employee to accept responsibility for his or her own career development by setting up career development workshops for them. In these workshops the employees complete works sheets much like the 'job history' and 'life history' forms presented earlier, and design action plans for their personal development.

Such workshops will not only assist you in identifying your knowledge, skills and values, but will also let you know that you are not alone in your career development needs. A bonus for the organisation is that employees often find they have far better opportunities within their organisation than outside it.

Manager-employee career counselling sessions

One of the best ways your supervisor or manager can help you with your career development is to help you with career planning. He or she can help you to:

1. Determine whether your organisational goals are realistic.
2. Identify your strengths and determine whether those strengths are important for future positions.
3. Identify areas of needed improvement.
4. Communicate career job alternatives.
5. Create action plans for continued development covering both strengths and needs.

Now let's look at some important strategies to guide you in your career counselling session.

The career counselling interview

In this section we will explain an eight-step procedure for participating in a career counselling session with your manager or supervisor, describing each step in detail. The eight key steps are as follows:

1. Prepare for the meeting.
2. Open the interview.
3. Present your perceptions of your knowledge, skills and values.
4. Ask for feedback on your perceptions.
5. Explore career choice alternatives.
6. Create an action plan.
7. Conclude the interview.
8. Follow up.

1. Prepare for the meeting

Make an appointment with your boss
Not only should you prepare for your career counselling meeting, but your supervisor or manager should do so as well. Therefore, arrange with your boss for a one-hour appointment in about two to three week's time. Tell him or her that you would like to discuss your career goals and get some ideas on the kinds of developmental activities you should undertake. Ask him or her to think about any special jobs or tasks that would be appropriate for you, particular training opportunities that might exist, and also ways of making your present job more challenging.

Tell your boss that you will make every effort to be honest about areas of needed improvement, as well as strengths; but that you would like feedback and help as well. Inform your manager or supervisor that your objectives are to determine:

- whether or not your career goals are realistic
- what the organisation needs in the future and how you can best contribute to those needs
- what skills are required for these future positions.

In addition, tell him or her that you will bring to the meeting an analysis of your own job and life skills and interests as well as a tentative action plan for reaching your career goals.

Fill in the job and life history forms

After setting a meeting date with your supervisor or manager, fill in both the job history and life history forms. These forms will help you to identify your knowledge, skills, and abilities, and also enable you to determine the kinds of things you really enjoy doing, as well as those you don't.

Use the job history form to list five jobs or positions you've held in the past, starting with your present job and working backwards. Use the life history form to list significant events in your experience.

Develop alternative career goals

Next, consider your talents and skills, as well as the things you like and don't like doing, and decide where you want to be in the future. Within reason, the more alternative career goals you bring to your counselling sessions to examine, the better your decisions will be. This means looking ahead at many possibilities, including job enrichment in your present job, special projects, or lateral moves for more exposure or challenge.

A good strategy is to make up a list of possible career goals. The idea is to create a list of goals on paper without judging whether or not they can be achieved. When your list is complete, delete those goals that seem impractical, combine the remaining ones where possible, and even add to the list new ideas that come to mind.

Create a career plan

When you have identified the direction you would like to go (even tentatively), begin to develop a step-by-step plan to reach your goal. A career goal planning work sheet is given on pages 147–148. Make several copies of this work sheet for use in your planning.

As an example of step-by-step planning, you may recall that I moved from a corporate job to my own consulting firm. In planning this career change, I wrote the following plan:

	Date to be completed
1. Discuss with spouse.	15 January
2. Analyse my marketable strengths.	16 January
3. Take a week's holiday and determine market potential by confidential meetings with ten key potential clients.	1 February

4.	Meet several other key successful consultants. Ask each one, 'If I do this, what can go wrong?'	1 February
5.	Determine equipment that will be needed.	15 February
6.	Project yearly business and family expenses.	25 February
7.	Locate resource people (ie, chartered accountant, bookkeeper, solicitor, banker)	15 March
8.	Locate sources of funds.	15 April
9.	Give notice at work.	1 May
10.	Select a replacement for my job.	15 May
11.	Select ten key accounts and visit them for an analysis of their needs.	1 June
12.	Design a mailing for all prospective clients and announce my availability.	1 July
13.	Follow up mail responses with phone calls and meetings where appropriate.	

Analysing risk

Notice the key question in Step 4 of my plan: 'If I do this, what can go wrong?' This is an important question that you need to ask yourself and others, as you prepare your plan. The idea is to try to develop preventive and contingency actions you can take if problems occur. Preventive action includes those things you can do now to reduce the probability a problem will occur. Contingency action is what you will do to stablise your plan if the problem occurs anyway.

You may wish to develop several tentative career plans for your meeting with your supervisor or manager. One is your primary plan. The others can be used if your primary plan proves to be unrealistic for your organisation.

Your career plan is tentative at this point. To implement a plan, it must meet not only your needs, but the organisation's needs as well.

2. Open the interview

The day of your interview with your supervisor or manager has arrived. Take paper and pencil, your completed job history and life history forms, and your career goal planning work sheet. You will probably feel a little nervous. This is natural – but you have come well prepared. You have given it considerable thought and organised planning and committed it to writing to make your discussion easier. In other words, you have done your homework and are prepared to take charge of your meeting.

3. Present your perceptions of your knowledge, skills and values

Now you will begin the process of giving important personal information to your supervisor or manager. A good way to start is to summarise your strengths highlighted in your job history form, and indicate the types of task that have been satisfying and dissatisfying for you. Then you will turn to your life history form and review your knowledge, skills, and values. (Summarise your findings by reviewing only the most important events, skills, abilities and values.)

4. Ask for feedback on your perceptions

At this point you will need to stop talking and listen. Ask your supervisor or manager how he or she feels about your analysis. What else should be added, both in the areas of strengths and needs?

You must not become defensive if your boss gives some feedback that seems uncomplimentary. Your job at this point is to listen. It is all right to ask questions if you don't understand what is said; or to ask for examples. But your goal is to listen with understanding. What you need here is additional information. You will not get it if you do all the talking or become defensive.

5. Explore career choice alternatives

In this step, you will present and discuss your career goal choices. It is to your benefit to have several career alternatives already identified and ready for discussion. (Do not present your action plans until the next step, since some of your goal statements may not prove feasible when examined.)

If a promotion is included in your goals, you may need to stress the need for open, honest answers. Some bosses find it difficult to be honest when there is a lack of promotional opportunity because they fear it will lower morale or upset employees.

Again, here you need to listen without interruption. Take notes if needed; and ask for clarification if you don't understand a response.

6. Create an action plan

When you arrive at an agreement on your career goal or goals, the next step is to discuss the tentative action plans on your career goal planning work sheet. You cannot do this, of course, if you and your boss have been unable to reach agreement on your goals. In most cases, however, you will find that there is some match between what you want to do and what your supervisor or manager can support. If so, you will now show him or her your tentative action plan and request help in evaluating it.

Ask your supervisor or manager for ideas on additional steps needed in your plan, and advice on any potential problems he or she sees. The goal of this discussion should be a solid action plan that has his or her support and a good chance of working.

7. Conclude the interview

To conclude the interview, tell your supervisor or manager that you are committed to making your plan work, and that you would appreciate his or her ongoing assistance. Finally, thank him or her for the time and thought given to this meeting.

8. Follow up

We sometimes begin with the best of intentions, and then experience problems because we don't follow our plan through. You will increase the probability of achieving the goal you have agreed if you set a follow-up date with your supervisor or manager. The purpose of this future meeting is to discuss your progress towards completing your plan, and to deal with any new problems that may have occurred.

Conclusion

The career counselling interview is only the beginning of an ongoing way of managing your life in order to reach your goals. Don't put your plans in your desk drawer and forget them. Look at them at least 52 times a year. Career development is *your* responsibility, not anyone else's. It is up to you to make your plans work!

Job history (page 1)

1. JOB	2. MAJOR TASKS	3. SATISFACTION LEVEL 5 High 1 Low	4. WHY DID YOU LIKE OR DISLIKE THIS SPECIFIC TASK? (For only the highest and lowest satisfaction levels — 5 and 1.)

Job history (page 2)

1. JOB	2. MAJOR TASKS	3. SATISFACTION LEVEL 5 High 1 Low	4. WHY DID YOU LIKE OR DISLIKE THIS SPECIFIC TASK? (For only the highest and lowest satisfaction levels — 5 and 1.)

5. WHAT GENERALISATIONS (THEMES) CAN YOU MAKE ABOUT YOURSELF FROM YOUR JOB ANALYSIS? THAT IS, WHAT ARE THE KEY THINGS YOU WANT IN A JOB AND WHAT DO YOU WISH TO AVOID?

Life history (page 1)

1. POSITIVE EVENTS (minimum of 5)	2. LIST YOUR SKILLS/ABILITIES (THAT YOU ENJOY) THAT RESULTED IN THIS EVENT.	3. WHY WAS THIS EVENT IMPORTANT TO YOU? (Be honest and specific.)

Life history (page 2)

1. POSITIVE EVENTS (minimum of 5)	2. LIST YOUR SKILLS/ABILITIES (THAT YOU ENJOY) THAT RESULTED IN THIS EVENT.	3. WHY WAS THIS EVENT IMPORTANT TO YOU? (Be honest and specific.)

4. FROM 2 ABOVE, LIST YOUR MOST IMPORTANT SKILLS AND ABILITIES.	5. FROM 3 ABOVE, ANALYSE THE REASONS WHY THESE EVENTS WERE PERSONALLY IMPORTANT TO YOU AND SEE IF YOU CAN IDENTIFY YOUR UNDERLYING VALUES.

Career goal planning
Work sheet

1. **Write your goal statement** ______________________________

____

2. **List the steps of your plan to achieve this goal**
   1. ____
   2. ____
   3. ____
   4. ____
   5. ____
   6. ____
   7. ____
   8. ____
   9. ____
   10. ____

3. **Identify the step(s) with the highest risk of encountering problems (critical steps), and mark with an asterisk**

4. **List the potential problems you see with the critical steps (what can go wrong?)**

Potential problems with critical step __.	P	S	Potential problems with critical step __.	P	S
____________	____	____	____________	____	____
____________	____	____	____________	____	____
____________	____	____	____________	____	____
____________	____	____	____________	____	____
____________	____	____	____________	____	____

5. **Rate each potential problem as to its probability (P) and seriousness (S), using H = High, M = Medium, L= Low**

6. **Analyse each high priority (H-H, H-M, M-H) potential problem as to:**

Likely causes	**Preventive action for each cause**	**Contingency action for each cause**

7. **Repeat Steps 4–6 with any other high risk critical step (refer to Step 2).**

8. **Incorporate key preventive and contingency actions into your initial plan (Step 2) as additional steps required.**

Chapter 12
Meeting Change Creatively

Change causes problems. In fact, the field of problem-solving states that all problems are the product of change. Change causes *you* problems! So not only do you have to deal with external problems resulting from change, you must also deal with the emotions – fear, anxiety and worry – that result from the changes you make to alter your life.

These emotions usually come from apprehension about the unknown. You're not sure what's coming. Or whether you can handle it. And you may fear that you are going to be less comfortable when it comes.

Human beings have different tolerances for change. While some feel overwhelmed by even the thought of making a change, others seem to thrive on change. Whatever your tolerance, this chapter is for those who must cope with change. It will show you how to increase your tolerance to change, and how to manage it to your benefit.

Many changes are positive ones. But sometimes changes don't seem to benefit you directly. In fact, you may even conclude that a change leaves you with fewer benefits, and that the change is something you are going to have to put up with.

Your ability to *manage* change is linked to your feeling of being in control. It is also linked to the personal benefits you experience in making a change. Your challenge is to discover the ways in which a change will benefit you. Or, if there are no apparent benefits, to find strategies to control the effects of the change.

Using force field analysis to manage change

I used to write books longhand. And then came computers. Talk about major change! So I bought the simplest word processing program I could find, and sat down to use it. The instructions were obviously written by a computer expert, who used words I had never heard of to explain things I couldn't picture. I became so frustrated that I almost gave up. The fact that the word processing program had a built-in spell-checker to help me overcome my spelling problem was the only reason I stuck with it – and finally learned how to use it.

Let's use my example of the work processor computer program to illustrate the use of what is called 'force field analysis' (see Chapter 7) as a tool to help me analyse change – both in order to gain personal control over the changes and to bring possible benefits of change (sometimes unperceived at first) into the present.

The first step is to list all the reasons – or 'forces' – that support the change on one side of a vertical line, and all the opposing forces (reasons against changing) on the other side. Then use opposing arrows to represent the competing forces, with longer arrows indicating stronger forces.

Force field analysis

Changing from longhand to word processor

Forces (reasons) for changing	Forces (reasons) against changing
	Anxiety over not knowing how to use it
Much faster	Initial learning time required
Fewer spelling errors	Cost of program
Don't want to appear 'behind the times' to my staff	Fear of appearing slow to learn
Easier to make changes in a document	Lost data when power is out
Electronic storage takes less space	

Now that I've learned how to use a word processor, I'll never go back to writing in longhand. But note that I had an overwhelming reason (my need for the spell-checker) to continue my efforts to master this new process.

Force field analysis helped me to decide to make the change by graphically showing me all the factors that influenced my feelings about the change. I could see at a glance all the positive reasons for accepting the change, as well as the ones against it. Next, I could begin to minimise the opposing forces with specific actions. For example, I could reduce the learning time required by getting somebody who knew how to use this program to show me how to. His help also reduced my anxiety over not knowing how to use this new program – as well as my fear of looking like a slow learner.

A force field chart will help you to deal openly with your feelings about a change. It can also increase your acceptance of the need to change. This technique is especially helpful if you have to cope with changes that appear to have little value. Accept the possibility that people had what they believe are good reasons for change (no matter how idiotic they might seem to you). Your job then is to uncover the reasons for change, as well as the possible benefits.

To tackle a specific change in your life, start by sketching a force field chart like the one above. Then write in as many benefits and disadvantages as you can think of. If the benefits side looks sparse to you, there may be some additional reasons why the change was introduced. Get more information. Ask your boss. Enquire from peers whose opinions you respect. Talk to others outside your organisation (if the changes are not confidential) to get their views.

And remember your goal here: to discover, if possible, additional *positive* reasons for the change – not to affirm your own discomfort with it. Find out reasons for change so that you can support the change, if possible, from a knowledgeable position.

If you can support, or at least accept, the need for a change through knowledge, your next step is to look for ways to control the opposing forces coming from the change. That will help you to cope with the changes – constructively, creatively and even, as is often done, to your advantage.

Causes for change

Being motivated to accept change is only the first step. Once we say, 'I see the need for this change,' the next thing we must do is to work out how and what we must change. And how we implement our personal changes depends on the kinds of larger change we are facing.

External change

External changes originate outside your organisation. These are the ones that can cause you the most mental distress, because they often cause a feeling of loss of control. For example, if the economy becomes depressed, and your organisation starts to lay off its workers, it can be difficult to feel you are in control of your future.

There are five major causes of external change:

1. New technology
2. Government regulations
3. Variable economy
4. Job mobility
5. Personal relationships.

Let's look at each of these causes of external change.

New technology can cause havoc within any organisation. Although it is rare that new technology results in industry-wide layoffs, it can cause great disruption in a particular organisation. Even if you don't lose your job, you may still feel anxiety over the possibility of being retrained, or moving to another job.

However, new technology can result in a job that is even more secure. Suppose your organisation, for example, decides to reorganise its reporting procedures, and therefore installs a new system of computers to speed the flow of information. As a result, you are given hundreds of hours of training to teach you how to use the new equipment. This additional training and your new skill make you even more valuable to your organisation than before.

Government regulations can also have a high impact on organisations. Tax regulations, industrial waste regulations, sewage disposal guidelines and safety regulations are all examples of laws and regulations that have caused major changes and resulting problems within organisations.

But even changes in government regulations can result in opportunities. As an example, look at what has happened to the car industry. Continued change in the government's regulations with regard to petrol has resulted in the development of high-efficiency engines that are among the best in the world. The net effect of this has been to help to save jobs by making the country more competitive in the world market.

Variable economy. Inflation, stagnation, depression, Third World debt, balance of payments, national debt and competition from the world market are all economic realities of our time. Since you have little chance of preventing any of these problems, the way to reduce your anxiety about them is to take action in advance to protect yourself when they occur.

Note that I said 'when', and not 'if', they occur. Large-scale economic changes have happened, are happening, and will continue to happen. As you know that you will experience some, or even all, of the global economic problems mentioned, and that they will have a profound effect on your organisation, then it is to your benefit to do those things now that will help you to cope with a problem when it occurs. For example, increase your savings. Cut back on high-interest credit accounts. Reduce your expenses. Get a part-time job and save the extra money.

Make yourself even more valuable to your organisation by increasing the quality and quantity of your output. Add to your knowledge and skills so you can do other, more secure, jobs. The employees who survive swings in the economy are those who are the least dispensable to their organisations. You'll find it is much easier to make such changes in your personal situation now than after trouble comes.

Job mobility has both positive and negative consequences. It is nice to be able to move from an organisation that is in trouble to one that is thriving. But such a move can also be traumatic. New bosses and associates, new procedures and policies, or simply new locations can all add up to stress.

Change is best managed by preparation. For instance, if you decide to move to a new organisation, the following are some of the important things you can do. If you belong to a professional society, become more active. Arrange, if possible, to talk to people who work (or used to work) in the new organisation. You can also contact the personnel department of the new organisation and ask for a brochure or pamphlet on the history of the organisation. If such information is not available in writing, ask for the name and telephone number of an older employee and phone him or her and ask questions about the company. Such a contact is invaluable in that you can learn about the organisation and the unwritten dos and don'ts.

You may even find it possible to ask your prospective boss to give you information on the people you will be working with – eg, what they do in their jobs, how they will overlap with you, and even their hobbies and outside interests. This will help you to establish links of interest so that when you arrive it will be easier to make friends. In other words, the more you know about your future job, the organisation, and the people you will be working with, the more comfortable and effective your transition will be.

Personal relationships. The final major external factor causing change – one which we must all cope with – is personal relationships. Marital problems, separation, divorce, alcohol- or drug-dependent family members, children leaving home, death – are all examples of external situations that can cause untold stress and change in our lives. The best advice in dealing with such changes is to get professional help; and, if possible, group support. It is far better to seek help than to try and see it through by yourself. There are many things you can do personally to cope positively with severe stress in personal relationships, but experience shows that trained resource people outside the situation are often required for success.

Internal change

External forces cause internal organisational changes – sometimes sweeping ones. But other changes within an organisation are caused by internal initiatives. These actions fall into three categories: personnel changes, job changes and organisational changes. Let's look at each of these in turn.

Personnel changes can have a strong impact on our ability to cope. Suppose you get a new boss; or a good friend leaves the organisation; or a new employee is taken on and assigned to work with you. All these changes can be difficult to manage.

When bosses change, people understandably become apprehensive. What will the new boss be like? What will be his or her expectations of you? Even if your old boss was worthy of first prize as the Worst Boss of the Year, you may still feel concern about what the new boss will be like. And, of course, it is even worse if you had an extremely good relationship with your old supervisor or manager.

There are always things you can do to cope constructively with personnel changes. For example, new bosses have histories – they come from somewhere. The odds are that your new boss was promoted from within your organisation. If so, it is fairly easy to talk to his or her previous employees and obtain information to fill in some of the unknown picture. You can even take the initiative and set up a meeting with your new supervisor or manager. In this meeting, tell him or her about your job tasks, and decide how these tasks fit into the overall work of the department or section. Then ask for feedback.

Losing a friendly colleague can also be distressing. In general, close relationships that develop on the job do not normally continue when one of the individuals leaves. You have at least two options in managing the change that occurs when a colleague who is also a friend leaves your area or organisation. First, the two of you can deliberately plan outside activities, or develop common interests that have nothing to do with work. This will allow you to maintain a continuing relationship, even though you no longer work together.

Or if you find you must give up the relationship, it is important to permit yourself to grieve over the loss. For example, I once had a wonderful boss, an ex-rugby player who was a mountain of a man with a heart of gold. And I liked him a great deal. But because our boss–subordinate roles had not allowed for friendship outside work, we could not maintain our relationship when I resigned my position and took another job. I permitted myself to experience fully the sadness and deep sense of loss that this change brought about. And this open acknowledgement of my feelings helped – though I miss him still.

Another type of change occurs when an employee you don't know is assigned to work with you. If this employee is new, then your role may be to help him or her to learn the job. Or possibly this is an employee who was transferred into your section against his or her wishes. Probably he or she is anxious about the new job. Therefore, your role is to help him or her overcome the anxiety in order to manage the change as smoothly as possible.

Since you know this person is probably nervous and anxious about the new job, do not say, 'This job is simple. You'll catch on in no time.' Rather than relieving tension, this can make it worse – since by stating that the job is 'easy' you are in effect saying that the person is not very smart if he or she experiences difficulty. Better to say something like, 'I know most new jobs appear difficult. But I am confident that you can manage it.'

You can also help new employees to overcome some of their anxiety by finding out what their outside interests are. Then introduce them to others in your section or department, indicating 'links' of common interest.

Job changes can also have major effects on us. Such changes can range from the addition of a new job task to a new job due to promotion or transfer. They key word here is 'new'. The more a new job is unlike your old one, the greater your possible anxiety. So when you are assigned a completely new job, you can expect to feel anxious about it.

A key strategy here is to make all the tasks of the new job clearly visible. That is, ask the person who is responsible for your training to write out your job tasks on a sheet of paper. Then review each task with the trainer, and write out an on-the-job training plan. This will take some of the mystery out of the unfamiliar assignment, and place you more in control. It will help you to see that what, at first, may appear to be an overwhelming job is really a series of particular tasks which you are able to carry out.

Organisational changes often cause us deep concern about our future. Some of the types of change that affect our organisations, like external, technological or economic ones, have already been considered. But there are also internally caused changes that organisations make. They want to be more competitive, introduce a new product or service, increase their profit, reduce operating expenses, pay bigger dividends to their shareholders, or even simply look good in the eyes of the public. But whatever the organisational change, you are almost certain to be affected by it in some way.

There are several types of organisational change. New equipment, new processes, new policies and procedures can all bring about organisational changes – which may profoundly affect your job. The best way to meet such change is by being assertive about your right to know what is going on. Speak to your boss, the personnel department, or even your department's director. Most of our concern about organisational changes is due to our not being kept informed. The more we can find out the specifics of a change from informed people, the better we will feel and function. Here, of course, you must be careful about rumours. Organisational changes tend to produce strange rumours. So make every effort to obtain your information from those people who do know the facts.

Guidelines for managing change

Several guidelines stand out clearly when we ask how to manage change well.

- First, changes almost always have significant personal benefits. Your job is to identify these benefits and to use them to create within yourself a genuine, productive acceptance of a change.
- Second, don't become paralysed by change. Work out which aspects of the situation you can control and take positive action on those parts. Even the effects of a change that appear most negative can sometimes be turned to your advantage, when you take charge creatively in the areas you still control.
- Finally, seek the assistance of others. The simple act of talking to someone who is a good listener is sometimes all that is needed to reduce your anxiety to a manageable level and to free your tension.

And above all, even if an organisational change seems overwhelming or impossible for you to accept, don't give up your job in a huff! Give yourself time to manage the change.

If you still choose to leave your organisation, then take the time to look for another job *before* you resign. Most people find that it is much easier to obtain another job while they are already holding one. The plain fact is that, as a rule, you are more highly valued by prospective employers if you are employed, and less valued if you are not.

Again, remember the two major objectives in managing change: look for the benefits and take control. Overleaf is a work sheet to use for managing the changes that are affecting you.

Managing change
Work sheet

1. Write a brief description below of the change that concerns you.

   ____

   ____

   ____

2. Using the force field chart below, list the reasons or forces that support the change on the left side, and the opposing forces on the right. Place an arrow over each force, with its length indicating the strength of the force (reasons).

Forces for changing	Forces against changing

3. What information do you need to further complete the chart above?

   ____

   ____

   ____

4. Who has this information? ____________________

   ____

5. What are the major benefits of this change for *you*? ________

   ____

   ____

   ____

   ____

6. What specific things can you do about the opposing forces (negative results) that will minimise or even reverse their effects, putting you in better control?

____

____

____

____

____

7. What additional actions will you need to take to make this change work beneficially for you?

____

____

____

____

____

____

Chapter 13
Being Managed

In this chapter I'll give you commonsense ideas that you can use to enhance your relationship with your boss. And I have chosen to do this by looking at what I think bosses really want from their employees. So let's pretend that I am your new supervisor.

Now that we are working together, I'd like to tell you privately about my expectations. I have reserved this conference room, hung a 'Meeting in Progress' sign on the door, and asked my secretary to see that we are not interrupted. Would you like a cup of coffee? All right, let's get started.

First, and most important, I want you to know what my expectations are concerning the way I would like us to communicate with one another. Next, I will briefly review my expectations about work habits in this department. And finally, I would like to talk about your job. Oh, not your particular assignment – but what I want from all my employees as they work in this department. So let's start with communication – and talk about the way you communicate with me.

Communication

First, keep me informed. Tell me not only the good news, but the bad news as well. The worst news is bad news that was suppressed until the situation became a disaster. If you tell me the bad news as soon as possible, we'll have more time to handle the problem. This will also prevent my boss from hearing about it before I do. It's very disturbing to have my boss walk up and ask, 'What's this I hear about a problem in your section?' when I don't have any idea what he is talking about.

The next thing I need is to know that what you say to me is the truth. I know this may sound odd; but I couldn't be more sincere. Let's look at an example. Suppose that last night my wife and I celebrated our anniversary and didn't get to bed until late. Because of my lack of sleep, I overslept this morning. An hour late for work, I pulled into the car park, ran inside the building, slowed down as I saw my boss in the corridor – and said, 'Sorry I'm late but I had trouble with the car?'

Now if I had told this lie, it would have demonstrated how unimportant my own character was to me. And it would have shown how little I cared about my boss. As I see it, people who lie about little things will also lie about important things. In order for me to do my job, my employees must have the courage to be straight with me. I'll help you in any way I can. I'll stand up for you with management. I will always try to be a person you can count on. But please don't lie to me! I can't trust people who lie, and I don't want to work with people I can't trust.

If I ask you to do something and you don't understand what I said, please ask me to explain what I meant. I'd much rather try to explain something more clearly than have you get into trouble because I didn't do a very good job of communicating. If you don't understand what I say, the chances are I didn't communicate as well as I should have done. So it's no reflection on you if I have to repeat my instructions. It is only a reflection on you if you nod wisely while thinking, 'What in the world is he asking me to do?'

I also expect you to let me know what you need to do your job better. I may not always be able to do what you want. But I will listen with respect. If I can't do what you ask, I'll tell you why. Also, let me know what you like about your job and what you want to keep the same. Sometimes it seems as though all I hear are the complaints. It's really helpful if you tell me about the positive things as well.

I would also like you to have the courage to let me know how I can be a better manager for you. Like most people, I'm sensitive to criticism. So simply be tactful when you give me feedback. By that, I mean if I do something that makes you angry, wait and cool off before letting me know about it. But tell me when you think I'm wrong, or about to do something wrong. I value your opinion. And be specific. Try to avoid generalities like, 'You never tell me when I've done something well!' When someone makes a sweeping statement like that, I naturally become defensive. It may be true that I don't give enough positive feedback. But by using the word 'never', the statement is very likely untrue.

A far better statement would be to say, 'I felt good about the work I did on the Adams report. But when I gave it to you yesterday, I was disappointed that I didn't receive some positive comment on what I had done.' With this comment, you are not blaming or judging me. Instead, you are objectively describing a specific incident that occurred, expressing your feelings about it, and stating what you want. You see, most bosses don't walk around asking, 'How can I be nasty to my people today?' More often than not, we simply don't realise when we say something inappropriate. So if you can let me know tactfully, I'll really try to do better the next time.

Also, have the courage to let me know what you like about the way I manage. I know there are all kinds of labels for people who butter up the boss. But I'm not talking about flattery for the purpose of making points with the boss. I am talking about the courage to be able to say sincerely, 'I like the way you did that, because . . ..' This lets me know what you appreciate about what I'm doing – and increases the chances that I will continue doing it.

Instead of spreading a rumour, I trust that you will let me know what you have heard. This gives me the opportunity to check it out and let you know what is fact and what is fiction. Rumours can be dangerous; they can cause terrible morale problems. And because rumours are usually distorted versions of the truth, they have a special power to upset people.

To sum up these thoughts on communication, I want you to do just that with me – communicate! Communicate good news and bad news. Have the courage to let me know how I can be a better manager for you. If you don't understand a job assignment, ask me. If you need something to do your job better, ask me. In many ways you are much closer to the work in our area than I am. As a result I must depend on you for accurate, timely communication.

Work habits

What can I say about work habits? Come to work on time. Take appropriate breaks. Work when you are supposed to work. Do your job to the best of your ability. If you don't then I'll have to talk to you about improving your work habits. And do you know something? I hate having to discipline employees! I worry about having to do it; I feel distressed about what I'll have to say and how I'll say it; and I worry about how the employee will receive it.

In short, having to reprimand employees about poor work habits wastes both employee and boss time.

I once had an employee who had graduated at the top of his university class. He was really nice man, and could do almost anything. But he had a problem. He was supposed to be on the job at 9.00 am, but often didn't arrive until 10 or even 10.30. He would leave work to go and have lunch, and would straggle back an hour and a half later. At 4 pm I'd go to look for him and find he had left early.

About every two weeks I would have to sit down with him and talk about his working habits. He would assure me that he would improve. But several weeks later he would fall back into his old habits. That man ruined more of my days than I care to remember. Finally I was forced to admit failure and terminate his services.

So get in the habit of developing good working habits – even with jobs that don't excite you. And it's not that hard to do. Just take things one day at a time. Decide that you don't want the anxiety caused by not getting to work on time. Eliminate excessive break time and long lunches. In other words, resolve to give an honest day's work. After all, the organisation pays you, and it has a right to expect your best for its money. Keep your work area clean and well organised. And if safety is important in your job, make job safety your life goal. In other words, commit yourself to good working habits – to make both of our days positive and productive.

Your job

The last thing I want to express is my expectations about your job performance. As I said when we started, I'm not talking about the details of how you do your job. What I want to talk about is the way you and I interact around your job.

First, always try to bring me suggestions for solving a problem, not just the problem. Please don't just come and ask me what to do about a problem. Spend a few minutes thinking it through, analysing what might be the causes, and considering some solutions. Then when you come to see me, you can say, 'Boss, we have a serious problem with X. But I think if we do Y or Z, we can resolve it.' Look at problems as opportunities to do things differently and better.

Next, do express your ideas. There is no way that I can have all the answers regarding your job. So I am counting on you to think of new and better ways of doing what we have always done. There might be a reason why a certain idea won't work; and if so, I'll explain the reason. But as you're closer to your job than I can possibly be, most new ideas need to come from you.

Because you will know your work better than anyone else, I encourage you to plan. Take some time to work out what you want to accomplish in your job. Then write out several key goals and objectives and make detailed plans for each one. When you've done so, set up a meeting with me to review your plans. By doing this, you take charge of your job. And I can see better how to help you get what you need.

One last thing before we call it a day. *If you run out of something to do, I'll appreciate it if you come and ask me if there is additional work available*. It's very distressing to see an employee sleeping at his or her desk, or standing around with nothing to do and taking up other people's time with chitchat. My personal feeling – and I know it is shared by most managers and supervisors – is that to be paid for what we are *not* doing is simply stealing money from our organisation!

I hope you don't feel that I've been on my high horse! My goal in everything I've shared here is to help you to be genuinely successful in your job as we work together. By following these few important guidelines, you'll find that you will experience the pride and fulfilment of being a self-directed, respected colleague whom others – including me – will increasingly depend on. Good luck! And whenever you have questions, please let me know.

Conclusion

After reading this chapter, you might think, 'Yeah, but you don't know my boss!' And you are partly right – I don't know your boss. But I can assure you that if you do your best with even the worst boss, you are likely to see dramatic results. You owe it to yourself to give your job your best. And your best will amost certainly produce benefits – for your boss, your organisation, and for you!

Chapter 14

Conclusion

Why is it that some people feel their tea break is the best part of their day? Who started the myth that the only time you can feel good about what you do is when you're not doing it? Who said that work has to be dull and deadening to your spirit? Look at some synonyms for work: toil, labour, drudgery, grind!

Did history start this depressing litany? Maybe. There was a time when grim-faced men, women and children trudged off to dark, dirty factories for 60- or 70-hour working weeks. Work in those days *was* 'toil, labour, drudgery and grind'.

But not today! Not in this country, nor in most other modern countries. Times have changed. And it is time for the myth of 'work as drudgery' to change. Your work can be fun, not drudgery. It can provide pleasure and enjoyment, and it can give deep personal satisfaction. But only if this is what you want.

This book is for those who want to take pride in what they do and pleasure in doing their best. I have tried to provide you with practical ideas to use in making yourself even more effective at work. And as you read these ideas, you might have discovered common themes. These themes are my personal values, which form a foundation for the ideas that are presented.

So to summarise this book, I'd like to state my values. I believe the following things to be true:

1. Work can be fun! If I have to work eight hours a day, and only get two ten-minute tea breaks, then *work* should be the best part of my day – and *can* be!
2. I must take responsibility for myself. I can't blame my friends, my boss, the organisation, my country, the world or aliens for my problems. I have the power to change myself to cope more effectively with my environment.
3. What I do or don't do at work does make a difference.
4. Large results in my performance are obtained by many small changes.

5. Problems are really opportunities to do things differently and better.
6. What I think of others is often dependent on what I think of myself.
7. My job in life is to be true to myself and true to others.
8. What I think I do and what I really do are often different. Therefore, I need specific feedback from others to determine the reality of my performance.
9. I can learn more by listening than by talking.
10. I can learn more by asking than by telling.
11. My colleagues deserve my respect, courtesy and concern.
12. If I take my organisation's money for the work I do, then I owe it my best.

Maybe my values appear to be a bit old-fashioned. That's all right. I've seen old-fashioned values like these make people, organisations and countries genuinely successful.

Further Reading from Kogan Page

The Educated Executive: How to Advance Your Career in Management through Self-Development, Harold Taylor, 1991.

Moving Up: A Practical Guide to Career Advancement, Stan Crabtree, 1991

The One and Only Law of Winning, Bern Wheeler, 1991

Successful Self-Management: A Sound Approach to Personal Effectiveness, Paul R Timm, 1988

A list of books for managers is available from the publishers at 120 Pentonville Road, London N1 9JN.